2

An Unlikely
Journey

An Unlikely Journey

Journey

Waking Up from My American Dream

JULIÁN CASTRO

Little, Brown and Company

New York Boston London

Little, Brown and Company
Hachette Book Group
1290 Avenue of the Americas, New York, NY 10104
littlebrown.com

First Edition: October 2018

Little, Brown and Company is a division of Hachette Book Group, Inc.
The Little, Brown name and logo are trademarks of Hachette Book Group, Inc.

Certain names of people portrayed in this book have been changed.

Unless otherwise noted, all photographs appear courtesy of the author.

The publisher is not responsible for websites (or their content) that are not owned by the publisher.

The Hachette Speakers Bureau provides a wide range of authors for speaking events. To find out more, go to hachettespeakersbureau.com or call (866) 376-6591.

ISBN 978-0-316-25216-4 (hardcover) / 978-0-316-41988-8 (large print) / 978-0-316-42151-5 (signed edition) / 978-0-316-42150-8 (B&N signed edition) / 978-0-316-25217-1 (Spanish edition, *Un Viaje Improbable*)
LCCN 2018952316

10 9 8 7 6 5 4 3 2 1

LSC-C

Printed in the United States of America

This book is dedicated to every family who's made
their own unlikely journey.

To Mom
To Dad
To Joaquin
To Erica, Carina, and Cristián
And especially to Mamo

Thank you

An Unlikely Journey

Introduction

It wasn't yet noon on Father's Day 2018, but the heat had already climbed into the eighties. Alongside US Route 281 in South Texas, there are patches of scrubland that stretch far into the distance, and with the window down and the sun at the right angle, you'll swear they go on forever. I clicked the air conditioning off and let the hot air wash over me as I headed south into the Rio Grande Valley of Texas, which borders Mexico. I was halfway through the nearly four-hour drive, and I passed the time imagining how different my life would have been if circumstances for immigrants almost a century ago had been more like they are now.

I was on my way to meet a group of concerned activists at the Ursula processing and detention center, about a mile from the border. They were making the trip to protest the Trump administration's policy of removing children from parents who were apprehended at the border. One of the activists was bringing boxes of stuffed animals and letters of support written by

American children, but there was no illusion that these items would do more than provide temporary respite. Still, given the traumatic experiences those kids were going through, it was the very least we could do.

Because I was leaving so early that morning, my wife, son, and daughter had taken me out to dinner the night before to celebrate Father's Day. Carina was nine and Cristián three, and both had been happy to spend time with Daddy. As loved as I had felt being with them, it had been almost impossible not to think of the thousands of kids their age, only a few hundred miles away, who had been ripped from their parents. Babies and toddlers were reportedly being relocated to "tender age" shelters, and children were missing medicine and going weeks without a bath.

As I neared Ursula, my thoughts kept returning to my grandmother, Mamo. Psychologists warn of the trauma suffered by kids who are separated from their families, and I had grown up witnessing an example of the long-term damage. Even at age seventy, Mamo had still wept uncontrollably as she remembered being pulled from her dying mother and told that she was going to live with another family in the United States. By the time Mamo crossed the border in 1922, she had left behind two dead parents and a life of unrest sparked by the decade-long Mexican Revolution. The circumstances of that border crossing, though certainly different from the experiences of the children whom I hoped to visit, had left a lasting impact on her life.

Her unlikely journey had been the centerpiece of my keynote address at the 2012 Democratic National Convention, where I described the American dream as a relay in which one person's sacrifices—in my case, Mamo's—were vital to the success of later generations. Because of the difficult journey Mamo made, it was possible for my mother, and then my brother, Joaquin, and me, to have opportunities that she never had.

President Donald Trump's administration's immigration policy seemed designed to inflict cruelty on innocent children, leaving a very different impression of the land of opportunity. Regardless of political affiliation, there was a widespread feeling that an American ideal had been desecrated. This was a wake-up call for the nation.

As citizens came to the aid of noncitizens, I saw few examples of political grandstanding. The country may be deeply divided along partisan lines, but the seemingly instinctive response that I witnessed on my visit was that we, as Americans, are more alike than different. If the highest office holder in the land was going to implement a policy so flagrantly un-American, then Americans were going to push back.

Many began calling the policy state-sponsored child abuse, and this characterization, I soon realized, was not hyperbole. Outrage spread like wildfire as news anchors broke down in tears and airlines openly refused to shuttle children away from their parents.

When I arrived at Ursula, I was already sweating in the ninety-seven-degree heat. I walked from my car to the group that had assembled outside the one-story building where families were being physically separated. Protestors held signs, chanted, and gave interviews to the media, exercising the rights that generations of Americans have fought and died for, and they did it in a noble way. It was working too. People posted photos of transported children on social media; protests were held all over the country; and the administration started backing away from its zero-tolerance policy.

I met twelve-year-old Leah from Miami, who has an undocumented father. She came to the demonstration with her older sister, and the two spoke eloquently about the fear that their father would be rounded up and taken away from them. Leah and I walked to Ursula carrying a box of stuffed animals and handwritten cards for the children. The glass doors were blacked out and locked, so I pressed the buzzer on the intercom. A Border Patrol official answered. I introduced myself and said, "I want to leave some letters for the children who are here, along with some stuffed animals."

"Okay, yeah, we'll send somebody out there," came the reply.

The door remained locked, and the box of toys and letters was still sitting outside the facility when I left more than an hour later.

The drive home was a conflicted one. As a Mexican American, I had a common history with many of the families seeking asylum. The issue of immigration is a complicated and ever-evolving one, but so many folks forget that their own lineage can be traced to another land, another nation, to a moment when their family's survival depended on the empathy and acceptance of strangers. It's no secret that most of us came here because America represented a land of expanding opportunities, a place where one could reach previously unimaginable heights of success through hard work. Times and circumstances change, I realize. But while it's easy to talk about the

American dream, every once in a while we need to wake up and ensure that it is not becoming, as it did at Ursula, obsolete.

And people have woken up. Their thunderous and unified activism brought attention to an injustice against our nation's basic sense of self. We took a stand and a powerful step toward reaffirming the nation's belief in the American dream. Three days later, President Trump signed an executive order ostensibly to end the policy of family separation.

The volume of the protests was instrumental in spreading word of the lives that were being destroyed by our federal government. Listening to those stories, witnessing those heartbreaks, and seeing the faces of those children humanized the immigration experience in a way that summoned the collective compassion we as Americans have not only for ourselves, but also for our fellow humans—regardless of nationality.

My own family's history reaches back to a similar border crossing. I hope that telling that story can help show how inextricably woven the immigrant experience is with the American experience and serve as a reminder that immigrants are one of our country's greatest assets as we work toward continued American prosperity in the twenty-first century.

PART 1

Chapter One

It's vague where family stories begin, but my twin brother, Joaquin, and I have always considered August 1922 to be the start of ours.

A seven-year-old girl, black hair falling down to her shoulders, held her younger sister's hand as she followed the man and woman they'd just met. The dust that hung in the hot air covered the girl's worn black leather shoes and the socks that no longer stayed up. The group walked along a line of lush green bushes bordering the Rio Grande, an oasis in the desert and scrubland that stretched thousands of miles in all directions.

They paused at the foot of a bridge, and the man wiped his brow with a handkerchief. The day was not hotter than usual, but it was almost a hundred degrees and there had been little shade on the walk.

He whispered to the two orphans, telling them that they were almost there. He pointed across the bridge at a building, which had a wooden roof and a sign that read U.S. Customs and Immigration hanging on the side. The man explained how they would pass through and sign some papers before going forth into the new country. For some reason, the little girl would later remember the words "Eagle Pass" from his explanation of the international border crossing.

Four tall men in grubby, sweat-stained Campaign hats stood beneath the bridge. They all held rifles but put them down as they waved the four people onward. The seven-year-old stared at the leather ammunition pouches hanging on the men's belts. One man wore a knife that reached down to his knees, the sheath scratched and oiled from years of use.

Nervous, she stared at the border guards' knee-high boots, pants tucked inside and covered with dust. One guard wore his rifle casually over his shoulder and smiled at the girl. He tried speaking some Spanish to her, but she just nodded shyly, still in a state of shock over learning of her mother's death from tuberculosis a few days earlier. She wasn't sure she'd even stopped crying before the man and woman had explained that they were taking her with them to America, where they lived.

She squeezed her sister's hand and smiled at the man in the hat again. He seemed sympathetic but looked like a soldier, and she had seen too many soldiers in her own country already. The Mexican Revolution had begun in 1910, forcing thousands of families to flee the violence and political instability. A president had been assassinated, officials had had their eyes gauged out and lips cut off, and the president's brother had been tortured with a red-hot poker. The uprising against the dictator Porfirio Díaz would leave millions dead, including revolutionary leaders like Emiliano Zapata. The continued chaos left the country in ruins, and soldiers had been a constant sight in the little girl's life. She had heard about many of them being killed and buried in the coffins her father made. One day he too died in the confusion of war and was buried in one of his own caskets.

The guards in the wide hats spoke with the man and arranged some paperwork that was signed and stamped. They shook hands, and the friendly guard bent down and said something to the little girl and smiled. She liked the acorn band around his hat; it seemed to resemble something, maybe an accent, on a dress she used to wear when her parents were still alive.

The man who walked her into the new country said something in a language she didn't understand, then folded up the papers and put them in his jacket pocket. He reached down to grab her hand and pull her forward as he tipped his hat to the guards.

That was how my grandmother always told the story of coming to America. My twin brother and I called her Mamo, and she was a constant in our lives, always making us delicious meals and telling us Mexican fairy tales about misbehaving kids being eaten. She also drank forty-ounce beers, escorted my brother and me to see *Friday the 13th* when we were ten, had a child out of wedlock with a man almost half her age, suffered from depression and diabetes, made the best *fideo* I ever ate in my life, was pulled from school in the third grade and still taught herself to read in two languages, and once tried to kill herself. She was one of the most amazing people in my life, and the reason I know one of the most fundamental truths about myself: where I came from.

Born Victoriana Castro in 1914, in the middle of the Mexican Revolution, Mamo grew up in San Pedro, a town located in the state of Coahuila. Landlocked and roughly six hundred miles from the US border, the region is known for its cotton and steel production.

She'd tell us about her parents, and we always wanted to hear about how our great-grandfather made coffins. But talk of her parents often led to tears and hysterical sobbing. "They wouldn't let me say good-bye!" Mamo would wail, in the same pitch and with the same pain every time, no matter how many years had passed.

Mamo was never clear on how Mr. and Mrs. García of San Antonio, Texas, came to take care of her and her sister, or even on how old she was when she arrived. The paperwork stated that the Garcías were the closest living relatives of the orphaned girls, but they were distant at best. The question was always on my mind, but Mamo was unable to provide a detailed timeline of her early life in Mexico.

After Mamo crossed the border, she lived with one part of the García family, headed by Gabriel García, the man who had walked her across the border. Her sister, Trinidad, was sent to live with two García sisters a few blocks away. Gabriel's wife, Tomasa, cared for Mamo as she settled into her new American life, but that life was far from easy.

My grandmother arrived in Texas at a time when persons of Mexican descent were discriminated against in ways that often paralleled the experiences of African Americans in the

Jim Crow South. Throughout much of Texas, Mexican kids were forced to attend segregated schools. Restaurants and shops posted signs that read No Dogs, Negroes, or Mexicans Allowed, and segregation was common in movie theaters, parks, swimming pools, and even cemeteries.

Mamo's new family lived on San Antonio's West Side, an area filled with Mexican immigrants and refugees. Swaths of previously undeveloped land were studded with small, one-story wood-frame houses, each of which came with a dirt driveway and a tiny patch of grass for a front lawn. The new immigrants opened restaurants, bakeries, shops, and bookstores, and they started publishing newspapers and playing concerts. Together with working-class families like the Garcías, the immigrants formed a tight-knit barrio saturated in Mexican culture, faith, food, and music.

In addition to Gabriel and Tomasa, Mamo lived with their two daughters, María and Herlinda. A local musician, Gabriel played classical music at weddings and *quinceañeras* (fifteenth-birthday parties for girls) and sometimes performed on the local radio show *Gephardt's Mexican Hour*. The pay was low, but at large events, if it was late enough, Gabriel was allowed to take home the leftover food.

They lived on West Laurel Street, a mixed neighborhood of African Americans and Mexican immigrant families. Church attendance was mandatory, and elders were to be respected and never questioned. When Mamo or one of the Garcías' daughters broke a rule, punishment was harsh.

"You boys have it easy today," Mamo would tell us. "My guardian would take a long rod and hit me with it."

"Like a stick?" we'd ask in horror.

Mamo would laugh, then tell us that she got off lightly. "Some of the kids at the other houses had their heads held under water until they thought they were going to drown."

Stories like that would put Joaquin and me on our best behavior for a solid twenty minutes.

Discipline or not, life didn't get any easier for Mamo. She was taken out of school in the third grade to help around the house, and just as she was becoming a teenager, Tomasa, who had become like a second mother to her, passed away. Then the Garcías' daughter Herlinda died in childbirth, leaving Mamo to help care for the new baby, who was also named Herlinda and who would become Mamo's enduring best friend. By age fourteen, Mamo had begun a lifelong cycle of cooking, babysitting, and cleaning homes for others to make a living.

When Mamo talked about her childhood, it seemed like she was walking through a minefield of anger and sorrow. She could be laughing or talking about her sister one minute, then grow deeply sad the next as she thought about the loss of her parents or the social restrictions she experienced as she grew up in Texas.

I've always felt conflicted about how my grandmother's life played out. On one hand, the García family took her in, providing her a new life in America. On the other hand, Mamo was never allowed to thrive and explore opportunities to live her own life.

Mamo was forbidden from socializing with or dating boys when she was growing up, and it wasn't until the age of thirty-two that she had her first boyfriend. His name was Eddie Perez, a young man from the neighborhood. Details are fuzzy, but it was clear that Eddie was eighteen and Mamo was pregnant. If their age difference wasn't shocking enough, the out-of-wedlock birth made their relationship toxic for both families.

The Garcías did not sugarcoat. *"¡Vas a matar a Gabriel!"* (You're going to kill Gabriel!) Meanwhile, before Mamo even started showing, Eddie left San Antonio.

In May 1947, Mamo gave birth to my mother, María del Rosario, named in honor of the Virgin Mary. Seeing how much Mamo loved her new daughter, the Garcías threatened to keep the child if Mamo, now thirty-three, strayed from the house or became pregnant again. Eddie's family never acknowledged his daughter, and years later, when he reappeared in the neighborhood—some say after serving in a branch of the military—he showed no interest in getting to know her.

The baby girl who became my mother doesn't have any memories of Gabriel, who died leaving his daughter María the small, one-story house with the peeling paint on West Laurel Street and the mortgage payments. María became the first Mamo, since her niece Herlinda had begun to have children. Mamo García, as Joaquin and I would later come to know her, was only ten years older than our Mamo, but she'd helped raise her and Herlinda both.

María, who also lived in the West Laurel house, assumed her father's iron-fisted discipline. Her authority was so clear that Mamo, already a mother in her thirties, referred to María as her guardian. My mom, on the other hand, was not great at deferring. She could handle the raw spankings and ear pulling, but as a kid it really burned her that after punishment was dished out she had to kiss María and tell her that she was sorry.

Before she even reached ten years of age, Mom's determined

personality was almost fully formed. "One day the whole family was out walking, and this pesky dog starts barking at us," Mamo said. "We went to church every Sunday, and your mom kicks at the dog and yells, 'Dammit to hell!'" A family member reached down, pulled on my mom's ear, and swatted her hard on the backside. Mamo could not help but laugh now, but her daughter resented how she never stood up to the Garcías' overzealous discipline.

This rebellion was not without cause. My mom was creating distance, letting everybody know that she would not conform out of simple obedience. She saw that while the house was full of love and caring, it was *very* controlling. She was also aware of the different levels of racism in society and felt the subtle social pressure of the times holding her back. It was difficult for Mexican Americans to succeed, and Mom felt an obligation to push back and not kowtow to anybody, family or not.

In a town where Mexican American residents faced constant discrimination, the Basilica of the National Shrine of the Little Flower was a cultural refuge. Opened in 1931, the church had been founded by friars from Mexico and stood as a point of pride for immigrants, its impressive facade marked by wide white archways and stained-glass windows. A welcoming and beautiful place of peace and worship, it was also a source of employment for the Garcías when cash was tight. Mamo García answered phones in the rectory during the day while Mamo cleaned the office.

Mamo always had a lot of pride in working at the basilica, but she also hoped that the job provided more than just a paycheck. One time, Mamo and I were making a cake when I was a child, and we ran out of milk. Mom joked about praying for some milk, and they both laughed. "When I was your age and we had no food in our house," Mom said, "Mamo García, Herlinda, Mamo, and I would light candles and start kneeling to beg God that the money they'd made serving his ministries would help."

"And we always made it through," Mamo said, making the sign of the cross.

"Somehow, we did." Mom nodded in agreement.

Mamo may have deferred to her guardian in some matters, but she held her own when it came to her daughter's education. She somehow managed to save ten dollars every month to cover tuition for her daughter at Little Flower Catholic School.

The strictness of her home life prepared my mom well for the Irish nuns who taught at her school. The Sisters of the Holy Spirit and Mary Immaculate wielded wooden rulers like world-class fencers. Classes were small, and it was hard for Mom to avoid attention, so she learned to toughen up when the rulers came out.

Even as a child, I had to wonder about the point of Mom's story as she told Joaquin and me about the sting of the rulers.

"Oh, I cried at first," she said. "Then I learned how to grit my teeth when they smacked me. By my fourth month I wasn't even crying when they hit me."

"They hit you with rulers?" I asked, incredulous.

Mom spread her hands out wide. "Long ones!"

But in many ways, my mom's situation lacked the constraints experienced by other Mexican American children attending public school at the time. They were often punished for simply speaking Spanish at school. Many immigrant parents, who were treated dismissively, made sure their children learned to speak English first, if not English only. Kids like my mom were, and often still are, forced to develop unique ways of straddling two cultures.

At school my mom excelled academically and soon began to develop a sense of herself in the world. There was a stark contrast between what she saw as a future full of opportunity and the confines of Mamo García's strict household. Mamo was working on the other side of town by then, cleaning homes in middle-class neighborhoods. Herlinda had moved away, so Mom was left under the loose watch of a neighbor while the adults made whatever money they could.

Life in the barrio forced everybody to toughen up, even grandmothers. Mamo once recounted cleaning a house and then waiting at a bus stop in the dark. A man approached her and raised a piece of pipe, demanding her purse.

"This one robber tried to tug my purse away," she told me as I lay in bed. "I was at the bus stop, and he came up with a metal bar in his hand. He started waving it at me and told me to give him my purse, and I prayed very loudly and then hugged it close to me. He swung it down and hit me hard on top of the head. Then he just looked at me. I think he was waiting for me to fall down. I told him to go away and he kept looking at me and then turned and ran." She tapped her head where the pipe had hit her. "He didn't know what a hardhead I was!"

Mamo's work schedule varied depending on the families who hired her, and she occasionally took Mom to her cleaning jobs rather than leave her home alone. On those days Mom began to see startling differences in the lifestyle she led versus those in other parts of the city. Mamo and Mom cleaned houses for five dollars a day, and there was one disgusting job my mom had to do that she never forgot. A family's cocker spaniel was infested with ticks, and my mom was instructed to take it to the backyard and pick off as many ticks as possible. Later, taking a break on an elevated area of the property, she saw some rocks and began throwing them down at the parked cars in anger.

I still remember Mom nodding at the dinner table as she told that story, inhaling from her cigarette. Throwing rocks "was wrong," she said, "but I was just frustrated and barely older than you guys. That family was a bunch of jerks."

"They even made Mamo work Christmas once," she added. "They weren't aware of her as a mom with a family, even when I was there with her."

As a young girl, Mom's frustration at the differences between her world and the one inhabited by the employers was understandable. The rock throwing, though, was something different. The people who owned the house Mamo was cleaning, and those who owned the cars, likely were not bad people, but to my mom, as a little girl, the contrast couldn't have been more stark. I hope she had really bad aim that day, but something tells me she was pretty focused.

That contrast was also vital in appreciating Mom, who was already trying to broaden her horizons in as many ways as possible. She did recognize that she had to channel her anger away from damaging cars and into a more constructive path.

Mom's consciousness was awakening at school too, thanks largely to the civil rights movement. One time, she raised her hand and said, "This school is in a mostly black neighborhood, so how come there are almost no black students in our school?"

Another time, the class took a trip to the Alamo, a monument to the Texas Revolution that is arguably *the* sacred institution of San Antonio. Her hand shot up again to pose a question, and I have a feeling that the nuns were nervous when the tour guide called on her.

"Why does the story make it appear so one sided?" she asked. "There were also Mexicans fighting alongside Davy Crockett and Sam Houston."

Indeed, she was learning to throw hard, uncomfortable questions instead of rocks.

Mom filled her after-school time with school clubs, winning the election for class president, earning a spot on the drill team, editing the school newspaper—she even joined the drum and bugle corps. Mom was constantly searching for escape routes from the repression she felt at home.

In May 1965 Mom graduated from Little Flower Catholic School with nineteen other girls and six boys, ranking second in her senior class. What a difference a generation made. Mamo's life had been defined by what she had not been able to do: never learning to drive, never finishing school, never living in her own home.

Mom had no money when she graduated and no tuition fund awaiting her, but she was determined to attend college. Our Lady of the Lake University, a private Catholic school on San Antonio's West Side, offered a scholarship to the class valedictorian, but Mom had graduated second. Fortunately, the valedictorian announced plans to marry after high school, so the scholarship went to Mom; in the meantime, she had also researched and applied for another scholarship from the League of United Latin American Citizens, which she won as a result of her high grades.

At Our Lady of the Lake, Mom was cut loose from the restrictions of home. Her intense determination and scrappiness caught the attention of Dr. Margaret L. Kramer, a psychologist specializing in education, who was spearheading research on bilingual education. Dr. Kramer and her husband had been active in the Texas Democratic Party for years, and it was a natural fit for Mom to mix her interest in activism with politics.

For almost a hundred years the Democrats had enjoyed an enormous advantage in Texas. But in 1961 a Republican, John Tower, was elected to the US Senate to fill the seat vacated by Lyndon B. Johnson, who had been sworn in as John F. Kennedy's vice president. Tower's victory signaled the beginning of the Republican rise in Texas, which would culminate in over two decades of undisputed control over statewide offices.

But in most parts of the state during the 1960s, the real power divide was between conservative and liberal Democrats. Texas governor John Connally, a passenger in President Kennedy's limousine during the assassination and a man who had taken a stray bullet from Lee Harvey Oswald, embodied the party's conservative wing. US Senator Ralph Yarborough represented the liberal faction. Yarborough was a firebrand from Chandler, in East Texas, who supported all the civil rights bills. In San Antonio, another liberal, US Representative Henry B. González (who had also been in President Kennedy's motorcade), became the first Latino in Texas to be elected to Congress.

Mom wanted to be a part of this exciting change. She organized a chapter of the Young Democrats on campus—and then helped organize the Young Republicans. Why? Because when she initially petitioned the school administration to start the Young Democrats, she was informed that someone would have to start a Young Republicans club simultaneously.

"I asked around and finally found a Republican," she said.

Mom went on to become president of the Bexar County Young Democrats before taking leadership at the statewide level, as vice president for women of the Texas Young Democrats. Like a lot of young people in the 1960s, Mom was attracted to the Democratic Party because of its growing advocacy for civil rights and for expanded opportunities for the poor. The Civil Rights Act of 1964, the Voting Rights Act of 1965, the creation of Medicare and Medicaid, and much of President Johnson's Great Society came to fruition during her first two years in college.

But for Mom, politics was personal too. She'd grown up in a city with clear dividing lines: Mexicans and blacks lived on the east, west, and south sides of the city, while the north side and the suburbs were overwhelmingly white. When it rained heavily, the streets in the less affluent parts of town flooded and backed up.

Mom frequently saw examples of inequality, and she brought these up at meetings. "We all know how poor the sewer system is in the barrio," she'd say. "We just have to look out the front window during a storm and notice the rising water in the street. Neighborhoods on the north side redid their drainage system so they don't have to watch garbage floating down their flooded streets during every storm."

Dr. Kramer introduced my mother to Representative González and other Mexican American elected officials. A loose coalition of these officials and other activists met up each Friday at Karam's Mexican Dining Room, a landmark restaurant with a two-story Mayan statue out front. Leadership roles rotated so that younger members had an opportunity to head meetings and get used to organizing people. When Texas was considering lowering the voting age from twenty-one to eighteen, state senator Joe J. Bernal asked Mom to testify in Austin at the capitol. He had put "coach" on his campaign posters (along with legislator, teacher, social worker, and church worker) and looked like a 1950s coach, with his stocky build and close-cropped hair.

This was a jump to a larger stage, and Mom hesitated. Dr. Kramer, a doctor in psychology, after all, read my Mom perfectly.

"It's fine if you're too nervous. It's a big deal, and speaking in front of people is one of the most universal fears," she said, nodding to Mom. "And this would be a lot of people."

Mom took that as a personal challenge and traveled to Austin to testify. Only a few years earlier, Mom had been disciplined by María García and forced to say she was sorry. Now, people in positions of power were supporting and pushing her. She saw that underserved communities needed people to expand their opportunities and to strive for a better life.

"You have to make your future happen," Mom would often say. She never beat her chest, but she also didn't shy away from forging her own path.

Mom was intoxicated with this new world, and politics became an all-consuming passion. Reading books and doing assignments lost out to registering voters, giving speeches, and distributing political paraphernalia. Decompression came in the late evenings with beer and the companionship of friends and fellow activists. She ended her first year of college by losing the scholarships and becoming a work-study student. She held down three jobs in the library and the school cafeteria, still charging into the political arena while barely passing her classes.

In her senior year, she and other student activists temporarily left Our Lady of the Lake to follow migrant farmworkers from Texas to the Midwest, teaching them in the campsites. It was the first time Mom had ventured out of Texas, and she relished the experience. In Wisconsin and Michigan, she followed cherry pickers moving from one labor camp to another, spending days in the fields teaching and sleeping in tents.

After the program fell apart in Michigan, Mom reexamined her life's direction. Education as a means of increasing economic opportunity was the foundation of her political beliefs, so she returned to San Antonio and after graduation began teaching preschool in the Edgewood Independent School District, an impoverished, overwhelmingly Mexican American district on San Antonio's West Side. In 1968, Edgewood was at the center of a civil rights legal battle when a group of parents sued the state for routinely funding poor school districts at much lower levels than those in more affluent areas of town. The case, *SAISD v. Rodriguez,* reached the Supreme Court, which ruled against the Edgewood parents in 1973.

Having returned to San Antonio, there was no way Mom was going back to live in Mamo García's household after speaking to thousands of people, leading meetings, and traveling around the country. She rented a ramshackle house and had an open-door policy for all her friends. Her fiery energy was directed at political change as well as the occasional house party. Ashtrays were piled high with cigarette butts, and beer cans littered countertops.

One of those friends was a cheery academic with a mustache and ample wavy hair named Jesse Guzmán, a married man with five children. He became my father.

Chapter Two

When Joaquin and I were seven, I asked our father about his own family.

"They came over to escape the violence of the Mexican Revolution, way back in 1910," he said. "For some reason, they picked one of the smallest towns in Texas."

"The smallest?" I asked.

"Really?" Joaquin said. "Like how small?"

"Almost." Dad laughed and paused as something ran through his mind. Lytle, the town where his mother grew up, was a little farm community a few miles south of Castroville. "Lytle was a literal one-stop Texas town that only exists because it had a train depot," he said.

Dad was born in 1940, and two years later his dad enlisted and was shipped off to North Africa to fight in World War II as a member of the U.S. Army Forces. Dad's first real memories of them together were when his father returned just before Christmas 1945.

My grandfather returned from the war as a trained body and fender repair mechanic but also as an alcoholic. By 1953 my grandma had had enough of the drinking and took a bus from Denver, where they'd been living, to San Antonio to be with her family. She didn't yet have money for two tickets, though, so she had her twelve-year-old son, my father, take the bus by himself two weeks later.

He remembered riding the bus and getting off around midnight. "I waited and looked down the road, down the tracks, down the dirt trail. Nobody. And, let me tell you two, it's a different kind of dark when there are no streetlights. I walked down the street and made it to my grandma's house—it must have been around twenty minutes later. I was like a zombie, asleep on my feet, stumbling and tripping. I finally found the house and walked up the porch steps. I didn't want to wake anybody, so I didn't knock, and I turned the front door handle."

This was our favorite part.

"Nobody was home! It felt like a ghost town," he told us. "I was only twelve, and I think I would have cried if I'd had the energy. Instead I just crumpled right there and fell asleep on a beat-up old sofa until my grandmother woke me up after sunrise."

This was an unbelievable story that we asked Dad to repeat. It felt like a chapter out of a Mexican *Huckleberry Finn.*

Dad's love for his grandparents enveloped him, but that didn't mean life was easy. Some people take family vacations, but the Guzmáns took family trips to work on farms. One summer was spent four hundred miles away, picking cotton in the brutal Texas heat.

Even so, the trips were positive in the sense that they made my dad determined to seek other opportunities outside of farm work. Like Mom, he experienced how poorly farmworkers and cleaning people were treated and recognized that a lack of education severely limited opportunities.

He spent his teenage years in the barrios of San Antonio's West Side, moving often and sometimes staying in public housing. He identified school as his escape route and attended Fox Tech High School, one of the oldest high schools in San Antonio. A solid student, he was married and expecting a baby with his wife, Enriqueta, by the time he graduated in 1959. Dad attended San Antonio College for two years before transferring to the University of Texas at Austin, majoring in math and adding four more kids to his family.

He graduated from the University of Texas in 1963 and took a teaching job at St. Edwards High School in Austin. Four years later, he returned to San Antonio to teach fifth grade at Johnson Elementary School in the San Antonio Independent School District.

Meanwhile, he began dipping his toes into activism. In San Antonio, the Committee for Barrio Betterment (CBB), founded during President Lyndon Johnson's War on Poverty, developed ways to encourage Mexican Americans to vote, wedge into leadership positions, and run for office. This was the kind of activism that my dad had been looking for, and he dedicated more and more time to this cause as Enriqueta stayed home and cared for the children.

Mom was running on a parallel track. She attended and participated in party conventions, knocked on doors to explain issues, and handed out pamphlets and stickers, all while holding down a teaching job. Her activism increased after San Antonio mayor William McAllister appeared on the *Huntley-Brinkley Report* to talk about Mexican Americans in his city.

"Our citizens of Mexican descent are very fine people. They're home loving. They love beauty. They love flowers. They love music. They love dancing. Perhaps they're not quite as, uh, let's say ambitiously motivated as the Anglos are to get ahead financially, but they manage to get a lot out of life."

With lines like that coming out of the mayor's mouth, it didn't take Mom long to get arrested with fellow protestors as they picketed McAllister's business, the San Antonio Savings Association. Getting arrested for the first time was a rite of passage for civil rights activists, and for my mom it represented another level of commitment.

To identify as a Chicano meant to take pride in one's Mexican American heritage, but it didn't guarantee uniform views among members of the movement. Many of the men in the CBB (and later in La Raza Unida, a third political party) conducted their activism with a heavy dose of machismo. My mom and many of her female contemporaries were not going to defer to anybody based on sex or age or position, so they often stood out. The different Mexican American organizations met and worked together frequently, and my mom was at the forefront as one of the more passionate leaders from the Young Democrats at Our Lady of the Lake University.

At first, my parents were acquainted only through activism. Dad advocated for better education services for migrants and taught them at Colegio Jacinto Treviño, a college named for a Mexican folk hero and formed by Chicanos who felt their community was being underserved by the educational system.

La Raza Unida, formed in Southwest Texas in 1970, was founded on the premise that neither the Democratic Party nor the Republican Party adequately served the needs of the Mexican American community. High unemployment and dropout rates, low wages, and poor health afflicted most Mexican American families, and leaders of La Raza Unida, who were mostly young, determined, and idealistic, had had enough. They fundamentally believed in the democratic process and sought to elect candidates to local, state, and federal office to put these concerns front and center. Long before "identity politics" would become a pejorative, these children of the barrio rebelled against the injustices they'd grown up with and made a direct appeal at the ballot box.

My mother believed wholeheartedly in the cause. At twenty-three, Mom was already a civil rights veteran, possessing a strong and articulate voice during rallies and organizing meetings. In 1971, some of the Chicano groups identified four candidates to run for San Antonio City Council, with Mom being one of them. The four bonded as they traveled the city gathering support and scaring the time-honored establishment for the first time. The city had an at-large election system, which meant that everyone in the city elected all city council candidates, not just a person to represent the neighborhood.

Back then, very few minorities or women had the resources or name identification to win a citywide election. The lack of registered minority voters was made possible in no small part by a poll tax that lasted in Texas until 1966, and the city's election system favored an organization called the Good Government League (GGL), a political machine of mostly white businessmen. Handpicked GGL candidates had a lock on elected office, which meant control of city resources.

The CBB candidates saw enough votes in the barrio to elect their slate if they energized voter turnout. Mom went on a speaking tour, confronting an opposition audience at Trinity University one day and combing the bars of Guadalupe Street in search of voters the next night. Her campaign drew from the support of a tight-knit group of young Chicanas who were as committed to making progress as my mother. Blandina Cardenas, her former housemate, as well as Irma Mireles and Linda Valdez, who would become godmothers to Joaquin and me, helped organize Mom's campaign outreach efforts. By this time, my mother and the Chicano groups she was a part of had matured and were now focused on gaining access to power in government as a vital next step beyond their protests, pickets, and rallies.

The slate lost the election but still effected change, and the level of excitement in the city's West and South Sides was empowering. The election raised voter turnout and broke barriers for female politicians within the community. It also produced evidence for the Mexican American Legal Defense and Education Fund to use in a case, filed with the US Department of Justice, arguing that the electoral system in San Antonio was unfair because underrepresented minorities could not elect candidates of their first choice to municipal offices.

The election created momentum to build upon, and my parents dedicated more and more time to the cause, which led to a blossoming friendship and then a full-blown affair. In 1974 Mom became pregnant, and my parents decided to live together. Dad remained married to Enriqueta but moved out, leaving her to raise their five children alone while he moved in with my pregnant mom.

Mom was the chair of the Bexar County Raza Unida party and was volunteering at their event when she went into labor way too early. The day before we were born, Mamo had entered a cooking contest for *menudo,* a Mexican soup of tripe, hominy, and spices, and she won the grand prize of three hundred dollars. The next day — September 16, 1974, Mexican Independence Day — Mom gave birth to Joaquin and me, two tiny, premature identical twins. Mamo's prize money went directly to pay the hospital bills.

My parents decided that each one would get to name one twin. My dad named me since I came out a minute ahead of my brother.

"Julián, because it rhymes with Guzmán and starts with a *J* like my three older sons, Jesse, John, and Javier."

Mom drew from a more creative source.

Joaquin's name was inspired by the epic "I Am Joaquin," written by Rodolfo "Corky" Gonzales, an activist, amateur boxer, and Chicano civil rights icon. His famous poem captures the tension between cultural and economic survival for Mexican Americans. The subject of the poem, Joaquin Murrieta, was a miner and social bandit in the 1850s who became a mythologized folk hero for resisting racial discrimination during the California Gold Rush. The poem ends with a defiant resolve:

I am the masses of my people and
I refuse to be absorbed.
I am Joaquin.
The odds are great but my spirit is strong,
my faith unbreakable.
My blood is pure,
I am Aztec prince and Christian Christ.
I SHALL ENDURE!
I WILL ENDURE!

Because my father was still married, we were given my mother's last name, Castro.

During her pregnancy, Mom had been encouraging Mamo to move in with her, but her lifelong loyalty to her "guardian" family stood in the way. Once Joaquin and I were born, Mamo's affection for us won out, and she made the move. Our newly formed family—Mamo, Mom, Dad, and Joaquin and I—moved into a tiny two-bedroom rental house on the city's West Side.

My brother and I recall an essentially normal family environment, but it must have been surreal for all adults involved. My father had a wife and five children living across town, whom he still occasionally saw. Mamo and Mom both knew he'd left a crowded young family to start a new one. Then there was Mamo herself—a woman in her fifties who had finally stopped answering to a guardian.

It took two babies to slightly slow Mom's activism. She still volunteered and got in the front lines pushing for change, but her energy and time were now being demanded by two rambunctious and already competitive baby boys.

When my brother and I were still toddlers, Dad got a job teaching math at John F. Kennedy High School in the Edgewood Independent School District, the same district where our mother had previously taught. We moved to another rental about a half mile from the school.

We loved sharing space with Mamo. She'd tell us grisly Mexican fairy tales about kids wandering out and meeting doom in various ways and then switch over to a *telenovela*-style tale (like a soap opera) involving a flirting bus driver who called her Queen Victoria.

Even though the house was cramped, it felt like a home. Stacks of Mamo's sordid romance books and Agatha Christie paperbacks were leaning against the walls in our room. Dad would recline in his chair, reading and smoking a cigar next to his recycled wine bottle that now acted as a candleholder. I'd sit and watch the wax melt down and harden over the bottle as we listened to music by the Rolling Stones or Carole King on the record player.

My brother and I never passed up an opportunity to turn an activity into a competition and often a fight. At age two, he pushed me off the bed and onto my face, requiring a visit to the emergency room and two stitches. One time I pushed him off his bike and watched as he hit the pavement and tore up his forearm. For most of our childhood, people had difficulty telling us apart, but Joaquin and I spent a large portion of our young lives and energy finding ways to distinguish ourselves as the winner or loser.

Meanwhile, Dad would sometimes take us to Spare Time Lanes, a neighborhood bowling alley. A haze of cigarette smoke hung in the air, beer cans and nachos filled the tabletops, and sweet 1970s melodies competed with the banging and beeping sounds of the arcade. The circumstances of each game didn't matter, for it always ended the same way for Joaquin and me. One of us would trail behind and then the losing one would channel his fury into the most powerful windup possible, flinging the bowling ball into the gutter. Eventually Dad would haul us out of there when enough people staring at us made it uncomfortable to remain.

Outside of a competitive environment, my brother and I were steady companions. We would run around the neighborhood, a strange urban wilderness populated with trailer parks, abandoned cars and refrigerators, packs of roaming dogs, and eccentric folks. A man known as Pops, who lived next to us in a trailer, made a lasting impression on us by taking his recently deceased dog and trying to complete a backwoods-style cremation. It didn't work too well, and I remember the sharp rancid odor that drifted through the neighborhood that day.

Our new address was within walking distance of our school, and Dad often accompanied us in the morning. Joaquin and I started kindergarten in 1980 at Hoelscher Elementary School, which was conveniently located a block away from Kennedy High School, Dad's workplace. Although our last name was Castro, he asked the school officials to enroll us with his last name instead.

As much as I wanted to destroy my brother in competition, I discovered that I could also miss him once kindergarten started. The school's policy required twins to be placed in different classrooms, so we were separated, although classmates and teachers still had problems telling the two of us apart. A couple of times a day I'd repeat, "No, I'm Julián."

In those first three years at Hoelscher, we kept up the same routine. Dad walked us to school most mornings and sometimes back home when classes were done in the afternoon. And now that we were in school, Mom started to again invest more time and energy into activism and working on various consulting projects. Mamo was always there to greet Joaquin and me, and it must have been amazing for Mom to see her showing her love through cooking and caring for us, work she'd done, often in less-than-ideal circumstances, for most of her life.

Joaquin and I took in the trifecta of many Mexican grandmothers: religion, cooking, and stories. Mamo grew up Catholic in the days before Vatican II and held steadfast to the old customs. "A woman's head is supposed to be covered in church," she'd say as she put on a black veil. She referred to priests affectionately as *padrecitos* and kept an image of the Virgen de Guadalupe in the house. She prayed to various saints to intercede in our lives, but, as with many Mexicans, her *Virgencita* reigned above all of them.

Mamo would tell me about the families whose homes she had cleaned over the years, often with obvious affection toward some of them. It meant a lot that some of the women and even their children still called her from time to time to see how she was doing.

Mom left the cooking to Mamo and Dad, and he preferred everyone at his side when he sat down for dinner. I should mention here that my brother and I did not yet understand that Dad had another family and that our parents weren't married. They acted like a happily married couple, socializing with friends outside the house a few times a week. When Joaquin and I were around five they started taking us to these meetings, which blended activism and partying. They drank and laughed and organized rallies and voter-registration drives as Joaquin and I entertained ourselves at the pool table or with the jukebox.

School provided another opportunity for sibling competition. I *loved* earning higher grades than my brother. At Hoelscher, I'd bring home rows of As while Joaquin received Bs and even Cs.

Favorite football teams offered another arena for rivalry, and it was there that I made a decision that wiped out any academic advantage I had enjoyed. When we were growing up, the Dallas Cowboys were phenomenally popular. Joaquin picked the Cowboys as his team, so I had to choose a different one. I picked the Philadelphia Eagles, who had a tragic habit of losing to the Cowboys. Dad, my brother, and I would gather to watch Sunday and Monday football games, and the living room would become the scene of wrestling and cussing and crying bouts, mostly at my instigation.

Mom wasn't very interested in football and channeled her competitiveness into activism. Her run for city council in 1971, though unsuccessful, had established her as one of the strongest voices for Mexican Americans in San Antonio, and she'd chuckle when someone greeted Dad as Mr. Castro. But even more satisfying was the fact that Chicano activism had forced positive change. In 1975 Congress had expanded the 1965 Voting Rights Act to include Texas and Spanish-speaking citizens throughout the Southwest. Mexican Americans were considered the country's "forgotten minority" in the voting rights legislation that had previously enfranchised African Americans in the South.

In 1977, San Antonio buckled under federal pressure and let voters decide if the city should change from an at-large system of elections to single-member districts. The referendum passed, and now, instead of having to run a citywide campaign to get elected to city council, candidates could get elected in one of ten geographic districts. This immediately diversified the face of public representation in San Antonio. Four years later, Mom helped María Antonietta Berriozábal become the first Latina council member in the city's history. That same year, in 1981, San Antonio also elected its first Latino mayor in nearly 140 years, thirty-three-year-old Henry Cisneros.

From an early age, Joaquin and I were taught the importance of political engagement, and we attended rallies and were even pictured in some of the campaign literature. By the age of eight, I lost count of how many times I heard my mother tell me, *As a citizen, you need to participate in the democratic process. If something is wrong, you can change it. Your efforts may pay off in the long run, even if you don't get your way right now.*

But just as our parents' activism was paying off, their relationship began to falter. Dad was gone much more frequently now, and when he was home, my brother and I would sit in our bedroom and listen to our parents argue. One night, Mom brought us into their bedroom and sat us on the bed. "Your father and I are separating," she said simply. No tears. No anger. "But don't worry, you're going to be staying here and living with me." Mom, Joaquin, and I were about to become Dad's second "other" family.

Chapter Three

As Joaquin and I headed home from school on Wednesday, February 9, 1983, we didn't have the slightest clue what our parents' split would mean. Even though Mom had explained that Dad was leaving, I couldn't have imagined what it would be like without him.

When Joaquin and I walked into the house that day, the space felt empty in a whole new way. Before then, we had often walked home with Dad and then played out in the street, only stopping to fuel up on some of Mamo's chicken and rice or *fideo*. Afterward Joaquin and I would watch TV, and if the show was interesting enough, we'd stay focused on the screen instead of each other. If the program lost our attention, there might be some shoving or mildly insulting words, which would turn into a shouting or wrestling match. But on this day, we couldn't even muster the energy for an argument. While I remember feeling grateful to have a brother like Joaquin, the house, the family, even Mamo seemed different.

And now the morning walk stung. Even gloating over my brother's misery after a Cowboys loss wasn't the same without Dad, who was a San Francisco 49ers fan.

Mom did what she could to make the transition less difficult, reminding us repeatedly that the breakup wouldn't change how much they both loved us. Maybe not, but from an eight-year-old's perspective, not having Dad around sure felt like a lack of love.

Besides the emotional rut we were in, there was a financial one too. Money became even tighter. Dad's occasional and modest financial support was often a lifeline, but he had also had a shared credit card with Mom and had left her with that debt. While Mom had weathered financial insecurity before, this must have been different, and I remember watching friends drop off boxes of food at our door.

Before the split, Mom had begun a master's program in urban studies at the University of Texas at San Antonio. She'd study and then do the required internship with the city government and take the bus home after six. She'd eat and then silently sort the mail at the kitchen table, slowly opening bills and notices from collection agencies threatening action.

Mom would have been well within her rights to take Dad to court for child support, and I don't know why she didn't. I like to think it was to protect Joaquin and me from resenting Dad; maybe it was the fear that he'd just disappear if he began to lag behind in his payments. Mom had grown up without a father in her life, and that obviously affected her decision too. She and Dad came to an informal arrangement, and when things got too tight, Dad would bring cash or bags of groceries to the house. Mom was happy for us to spend time with him, and often even encouraged it.

One Tuesday a few months after the split, we heard Dad pull up outside. Mom announced his arrival, and Joaquin and I ran outside to jump into his rusted gray Oldsmobile. He drove us a few miles across town to his small, one-bedroom rental apartment. The light brown faux-wood floors made a funny hollow sound as we walked in, and the three of us couldn't fit in his tiny kitchen.

It was obvious to Joaquin and me that Dad's pad wasn't designed for two more people, but he had a TV, so that was good enough for us. Every Tuesday Dad would pick us up from school, and we'd hang out at his place watching *Who's the Boss* and *Growing Pains*. We'd walk across the street to an old-fashioned diner for cheeseburgers and Cokes. On some weekends he'd take us back to Spare Time Lanes to bowl, or we'd walk around Woodlawn Lake and pose for photos that he'd take with his new Pentax K1000 camera.

After a couple of years, his visits became more spaced out. Some weeks he was too busy, and other times Joaquin and I avoided the possibility of disappointment by staying home to shoot hoops with our friends. Gradually we grew more distant from Dad, but the separation was made easier by how close Mom, Mamo, Joaquin, and I had become.

One day, around the time my parents split up, Mom asked my brother and me to sit down after we got home from school.

"We're going to be moving," she said. "I found another two-bedroom house for us on the West Side, right across the street from your cousins." Mamo's sister, Trinidad, lived on Hidalgo Street with her daughter, Terri, and Terri's four children.

"You'll also have to go to a new school because we'll be zoned for a new district."

"Yes!" Joaquin and I shouted together. Our cousins were close to our age, and it was always a blast to hang out with them at family functions, but we could also tell how happy Mom was about the move. Looking back, I think it was an important change for her, in part because she was going to be out of the house that we had shared as a family with Dad.

The new school we would be attending, Carvajal Elementary, was a one-story beige brick building that had opened in 1949 and still looked like it did back then. On the first day, Joaquin and I walked the four blocks to school, and along the way we noticed that while the chain-link fences weren't as rusted and sagging as in our old neighborhood, the houses we passed were built in the same style: small, post–World War II bungalows. And just as many people here left broken washing machines off to the side of their gravel driveways as before.

But this neighborhood had something special. As we were moving in, one kid our age zipped along the streets on his bike. He slowed and checked us out, then biked across the street, hopped the curb onto the lawn, and dropped his bike to run inside. Five minutes later we heard the echoes of a basketball bouncing as he shot hoops in his small backyard.

Joaquin and I didn't care about peeling paint or how much overgrown grass our new place had—we zeroed in on the priority: a new friend. By the second week of riding bikes and shooting hoops with Eric, we had a new best buddy. Joaquin and I may have body checked each other over who used the toothpaste first, but we had no problem sharing our new pal.

Eric knew the neighborhood and showed us all the shortcuts while biking—the best place to jump curbs, which streets had crazy dogs that would chase you, and which neighbors were the cranky ones we ought to avoid. The three of us often ended up biking around together, looking for empty Coke bottles to exchange at Three J's convenience store for money to buy candy and soda, which we'd divide and enjoy sitting on a sidewalk in the Texas heat.

When we weren't biking, we were playing basketball with a nine-foot hoop drooping from a warped backboard in Eric's tiny backyard. A paved court was a luxury for the nice side of town—we played on packed, gravel-studded dirt with Eric and his brothers, Richard, Dennis, and Bruce. Dribbling was risky, since the ball bounced unpredictably on the rocks, so we became dependent on long shots from the back edge of Eric's house, which served as our three-point line. Rain turned the court into mud, but that didn't always stop us.

If we were really motivated, some summer days we'd walk a mile to the Calderon Boys and Girls Club and play ball in a real gym, shoot pool with other neighborhood kids, and get a free brown-bag lunch with a sandwich, chocolate milk, and graham crackers. To cap the day off, we would explore the drainage ditch behind the club before heading home.

One thing I didn't expect to happen after we moved was an improvement in Joaquin's academic performance. Joaquin had always been a mediocre student, but once Dad wasn't in the house, Joaquin's grades seemed to rise naturally.

"What'd you get?" I asked him when we got our first report cards from our new school. For me these moments had always been rich in gloating since I got better grades. I held up my report card to show him the neat rows of As.

"Yeah, me too." He held up his own report card. "Straight As!"

That signaled the end of my unchallenged academic run. Soon after, there was a math contest at school, and I was certain that I *killed* it on the test, so I taunted Joaquin.

The next day the whole school sat at assembly as a teacher walked up and gave a brief speech. Most of the audience had clearly already checked out, and it was only the math nerds feeling the nervous energy. Beating Joaquin was always fun, but doing it in front of classmates, with Ms. DeLuna delivering the blow, was almost too much for me. Ms. DeLuna did the usual teacher thing, congratulating everybody and talking about how impressed she was with our effort and willingness to stretch ourselves. Then she began to award the ribbons.

"Third place goes to Julián Castro."

That was a disappointment, but I consoled myself with the thought that I beat Joaquin. I walked up and received my ribbon. I could stick it on the fridge, and every time Joaquin saw it he'd have to reckon with my superiority, at least. Ms. DeLuna announced the second-place winner. Then she said, "And in first place, congratulations to Joaquin Castro!"

That ribbon cut deep.

I didn't even burn with anger or get emotional the way I did when I lost at bowling. This time, I went stone cold. I didn't even congratulate Joaquin. Nothing had ever embarrassed me like this, and worse, I hadn't even seen it coming.

We remained somewhat competitive, but the intensity of it gradually faded, and eventually we set aside firm beliefs in one of us being better than the other in certain activities. We'd evened out and won and lost in a much more random manner, which actually *pushed* both of us to exceed our own expectations. Now, sometimes I'd beat him at basketball and sometimes he'd bring home a better grade, but we always felt the other's breath on our necks, which made us find that extra boost.

And I did love seeing my brother grow in confidence at school. Joaquin and I have rarely spoken about our parents' breakup, but he did mention that Mom and Mamo created a much more lenient atmosphere, which allowed him to relax compared to Dad's stricter environment. A drop in parental pressure had allowed him to find his own way to succeed.

When Mom was busy at school or working at her internship with the City of San Antonio, she would usually leave Mamo to watch us, but sometimes she would take us with her to school.

The three of us would wait for the bus, Joaquin and I stretched out and bored on the bench even before we'd left the neighborhood. A bus would pull up, already packed with workers and students. We'd find a seat and rest for a bit before transferring to another bus. After an hour and twenty minutes, when we'd already flipped through our wrestling magazines twice, the bus would arrive at a campus the size of a small town. The campus was so far away from where most students lived that it had been mockingly dubbed the University of Texas near San Antonio. Like so much of the city's development, it was located in the northern section of town, away from the poorer and working-class neighborhoods.

Joaquin and I trailed behind Mom as she carried an armload

of books and speed walked through what felt like the entire 725-acre campus. The reward? We sat in the back of Mom's classes doing homework, reading, drawing, and quietly aggravating each other. At home, Mom ran a very loose ship in terms of discipline since Dad left, but she had her limits, and we knew that if we embarrassed her or acted up in school we'd unleash some serious wrath. By the time we transferred to another bus on the way home, Joaquin and I were zombies. Mom would find a seat and we'd lean against her and fall asleep until she gently shook us awake at our home stop.

Going with Mom to school was the most consistently boring aspect of our childhood, but even then it wasn't lost on Joaquin and me: *Y'all will be in an environment like this sooner than you think.* Mom knew how a degree expanded options in life. She loved Mamo but made it very clear to Joaquin and me on numerous occasions that Mamo's station in life was a direct result of her education having been taken from her.

That summer of 1983, Mom sent the two of us to College for Kids, a low-cost children's summer program at San Antonio College. Mom made it clear to us before the age of nine that we were going to college. I envisioned myself instead as a professional quarterback—which Mom said was fine as long as I had a degree.

Mom finished her master's program in 1983 and then started her first full-time job since having us. During her internship at the City of San Antonio, enough people had been impressed with her that she was hired right away as a management and supervision trainer. Within a few weeks she was already working on other committees that introduced day care for city employees, increased the number of women in the fire department, and improved mental health resources for employees. Once an activist, always an activist.

During school breaks and in the summer, Joaquin and I often had to hop on the bus with Mom and go to work with her for the day. We'd walk with her on the street until hitting the lawn and then running through the trees to see who could reach the Plaza de Armas building first. Mom worked in a building next to the Spanish Governor's Palace, which had served as a residence and office for leaders of the Spanish military command in Texas from 1722 until the early 1800s.

Mom brought us into her new office with its gray, low-pile carpet, which we soon discovered was unsuitable for lying on and would cause nasty burns on our elbows and knees during wrestling matches. The walls were painted the same off-white color used in doctor's and dentist's offices. Just like at home, Mom prepared her desk by putting papers and pens over all the available space. Her area always looked like an office set for a hurricane movie. The sign on the wall was all Mom too: a yellow-and-red placard that read, "God is coming back…and boy is she pissed!"

On the first summer day we spent with Mom at her job, Joaquin and I did some exploring. The trees in the courtyard provided shade to lie in, and the interior of the Plaza de Armas building had enough open space to fit our entire house. We'd run down the stairs where Mom worked, bouncing off each other to see who'd make it to the bottom first, and peer up from the basement into the middle courtyard and the windows of other offices. I'd crouch down and peer over the window sill, pretending to be James Bond or a World War II spy covertly scanning the activity above for suspicious behavior. There were some questionable characters, like the guy with the push-broom mustache who always wore a leather vest. But mostly our reports consisted of old (to us) people drinking coffee, leaning back on wooden chairs, picking up phones, and shuffling papers.

Into this environment wafted the distracting aroma of Panchito's, a local Tex-Mex restaurant, which operated out of the basement. Smells always rise, just like we learned in science, and the torturous scent of delicious breakfast tacos rose up through the entire building.

Two identical nine-year-old kids who had good manners were too hard for the employees of Panchito's to resist. They adopted us, and we developed a stray cat sort of relationship with them. They were beyond patient, and probably considered us free entertainment as we heatedly argued about whether Roger Staubach or Johnny Unitas was the better quarterback. The issue was critically important to us, cute to them.

During the summer we were there at least a few times a week. Mom would cut us loose and we'd run and spy and climb trees or read in the shade until hunger set in. We'd take the few bucks Mom had given us and walk into Panchito's and order bean and cheese tacos for breakfast. We'd sit at a table, relaxing for a bit in the cool restaurant before going outside to check out the goings-on around downtown and then return hours later for a lunch of cheese enchiladas.

At 4:30 Mom and her colleagues began drifting into the restaurant to unwind over beers. My brother and I knew well how to skip along that tightrope between cute and annoying, and Mom's coworkers were constantly buying us Cokes and tasking us with feeding the jukebox.

While a steady job provided more stability, it also meant an increase in Mom's anxiety. Truth be told, Joaquin and I sometimes made it worse. Mom routinely had to drag us out of bed in the morning (except on weekends, when we would practically jump out of bed before sunrise), and at least a couple of times a week Joaquin and I would nearly miss the bus as we fished around the house for Mamo's purse so that she could give us a dollar for Cokes and Nutty Buddy bars. At least three times a week, she'd be running late in the morning and unable to locate the purse and ask us to help. Imagine how desperate you have to be to employ two boys—who could barely keep track of their action figures—to find a purse.

Mamo's purse was old, made of dark-maroon faux leather. Joaquin and I would drop our books or toys and kneel down on the pockmarked hardwood floor to peer under living room couches and the beds in each room. We'd start flipping cushions, and usually found it stuffed into some well-worn crevice in the sofa. If we didn't find it there, then things got serious and it was time to pray to St. Anthony. As soon as one of us found it, Mamo would gratefully proclaim that her prayers to St. Anthony had been answered.

Answered prayers aside, it sometimes seemed that Mom had three kids instead of two, and she had a very complicated relationship with one of them. My grandmother loved Mom, Joaquin, and me profoundly, but she would occasionally criticize Mom in a way that grated on Mom, so Mom would criticize her back and we'd witness old emotional wounds reopening. Raising two sons while caring for Mamo ignited old resentments in my mother.

Mom never got over how, from her perspective, her own

mother hadn't stood up for her when Mamo García exacted harsh physical discipline for trivial offenses. Mom could deal with the punishment, but how her mother had tried to crush her rebellious attitude rather than encourage her to refocus her strong will was unforgivable. Mamo García had provided a stable home for Mamo and Mom, but she had also disciplined Mom relentlessly, and Mom was happy to escape to college and her own apartment when she came of age.

Mom saw in Mamo a refusal to take control of her life. Mamo had never learned to drive, always relying on the bus or others to get around. This reliance became increasingly problematic after she developed diabetes and needed constant shuttling to doctor's offices when her condition began to deteriorate. She hardly took her medicine, making things worse not only for herself but also for Mom, who grew resentful.

Mamo's ill health threw off the precarious family balance that Mom struggled to maintain. Dad wasn't paying child support, so it was already a stretch to make ends meet. Not having a car was also taking its toll on Mom, who had to figure out how to get Mamo to and from doctor's appointments while holding down a job. Sometimes when Mom walked through the door, she had a short exchange of sharp words with Mamo before retiring to her room, and Mamo would stay in the living room with us, wailing, "Your mother doesn't love me."

Kids can be very adaptable, so at first we didn't think there was a problem when Mom began returning later and later from work in a different state of mind—talkative and generally looser. Growing up, we'd seen plenty of examples of drunken behavior. Get a gaggle of activists together and start opening beers, and you'll see tears and shouting and occasionally a fight being broken up. Even Mamo popped a forty-ounce Old Milwaukee a couple of times a week.

One Friday, in the fall of 1985, Joaquin and I ate dinner with Mamo. Sometimes Mom didn't make it home by dinnertime, so her absence didn't bother us as we ran over to Eric's house and played a little one-on-one until it got dark. Back home, we watched *Dallas* with Mamo and then got ready for bed. Mom was still absent, and Mamo seemed agitated. While Joaquin and I sat reading in bed, a car with loud voices pulled up out front. A work colleague had given Mom a ride home, and it was clear from the laughing and loud bursts of slurred words that Mom was very drunk. There was no way she'd have made it home on the bus on her own. There were few things that embarrassed me as a kid—I didn't care if my clothes were worn or that our family didn't have a car—but I was embarrassed that night when Mom made a scene by refusing to get out of the car.

I looked at Joaquin. He was silent, but I could tell he was anxious. We were both sitting up and listening to Mom, and after a while we got out of bed and walked outside to the front curb.

"C'mon, Mom, let's go inside," Joaquin said.

"Yeah, we'll help you," I said.

She stank of alcohol in that way that people smell when they've marinated in too much of it for hours. I reached down and took her hand. She looked up at my brother and me and smiled. "I love you, sons," she said.

I did my best to pull her up out of the front seat. Joaquin helped steady her from the side as she stood up.

"I love you, sons," she said again.

"We know you do, Mom."

I put her arm around my neck and held it as Joaquin and I moved her forward, stepping carefully over the crabgrass patches in the skinny walkway toward our house.

Mom did a much better job of hiding her drinking from us after that. She did not sit us down to explain her behavior that night, but it really affected my brother and me. We could see that Mom was headed down a bad path, but we didn't know what to do about it.

Then her hair started to fall out. Joaquin and I began to notice large clumps of long black hair collecting in the drain and the corners of the shower. She often shared with us anything that our maturity level would allow us to understand, and this, she clearly felt, was one such subject.

Mom sat us down. "My hair is falling out, sons. I don't know what's happening. The doctors don't know what's happening, but—" she pulled back her hair to reveal a smooth patch of skin on her head, "—it's falling out."

She ran a hand through her hair and looked at the strands between her fingers. "It's just hair, right? The important thing is that I'm not sick. They did a bunch of tests, and my health is fine," she said.

It only took another week for her hair loss to become alarmingly obvious. We'd only known Mom to have straight black hair cropped at her neckline, but that style was no longer an option. Mom called Joaquin and me into the bathroom, and very much like an empowering salute, she held up an electric razor. This decision, at last, would give her some sense of control over her hair loss. She looked in the mirror and began running the razor over her scalp.

She smoothed her hand over her bald head and smiled at Joaquin and me. "How does it feel?" she asked, as we took turns running our fingers across her smooth scalp. I looked at Mom and smiled because she seemed happier. The next day was a Saturday, and the three of us hopped on a bus to a local mall to shop for a wig. It didn't take long to find a simple one with short black hair that looked passable.

Mom had involved Joaquin and me in something difficult for her, and it forever changed our relationship with her. It also affected the way we dealt with our own challenges. If she had hidden the problem and been ashamed of it, we would have learned that denial was the way to handle problems. Mom showed us how to face something emotionally difficult and not look away. From that point on, I never felt alone when problems arose. And looking back now, I realize that my brother and mother have been a part of all my major decisions. We didn't have much in the way of material things, but we were given an unshakable foundation of support at a very young age.

Chapter Four

Mamo's younger sister, Trinidad, was about the same height as Mamo herself—around five feet tall—with jet-black hair and a dark complexion. She lived across the street from us with her daughter, Terri, and Terri's four children. Having family that close not only made keeping an eye on me and Joaquin easier for Mamo but also provided her much-needed company.

My brother and I were quickly introduced to a whole new style of adult supervision. Trinidad's eldest son, Luis, had served in the army and owned a welding shop, and at twenty-four years our senior he often acted like our contemporary. A slight guy at five foot six, he made up for a lack of height with an oversized personality—opinionated and raunchy. He'd cruise over on weekends and often waved as he sped past Joaquin and me playing. One Saturday, my brother and I were biking around when we found a discarded piece of plywood. We hunted around the garage and pulled out two cinder blocks. I spaced the blocks on the floor, Joaquin dropped the wood on top of them, and we got back on our bikes.

After about four jumps, Luis drove up and watched us.

"What's up?" he asked. "Who is who again?" he joked.

"What's going on?" I responded.

"Drop the bikes and jump in the car and let's go for a ride."

We pedaled over to the yard, dropped our bikes on the front lawn, and hopped into the back seat, which was as big as a sofa. Luis took a few turns, and half a mile later we were on Guadalupe Street, a thoroughfare lined with restaurants and *tienditas* that bisected the West Side. Usually, we headed there to pick up fast food or get a haircut. Not this time. As we turned onto Guadalupe, we could see a block full of women wearing as little as possible.

Luis slowed down and cranked his window down. "That's a good one," he said as a lady walked over. "Ask her how much she costs."

I saw an empty space in between the front seat and back seat and ducked down there, face glowing red. Not enough space to hide from the woman teetering on too-high heels and wearing a skirt that seemed to reveal more than if she hadn't been wearing anything at all. She smiled. I folded myself up and began punching at the front seat.

"Let's go! Get the hell out of here!"

"Next time, ladies!" Luis called out before breaking into a wild cackle and driving off.

"You guys don't know shit from shinola," he howled, glancing over his shoulder at Joaquin and me as we continued to duck down in the back. "Talk to her next time!"

A few minutes passed. "Let's go grab some grub," he said

with a tone of resignation. Off for cheeseburgers from Ray's Drive Inn, our meal of choice.

Mom had attended sixteen years of Catholic school, and while she opposed corporal punishment and didn't regularly attend church, she had appreciated the quality and stability that a Catholic school education had afforded her.

She had not been impressed with Carvajal Elementary School, and after our second full year there, she called Joaquin and me in for a talk.

"Boys, what do you think about going to St. Mary's next year?"

Joaquin and I shot each other a puzzled look.

Even though it was posed as a question, we figured that Mom had already formed a strong opinion. Mom gave us a wide berth and rarely expected much of us other than good grades. I didn't know what a Catholic school would be like, but I remembered her telling us about the strict discipline. And the rulers.

"I think it'll be good for you," she added. "And it's right down the block from work, so it'll be easy."

"I guess so," Joaquin said. Right then, we hit on one of our most clever ideas. Mom was clearly happy with our reaction, but something more pressing needed to be addressed.

"Mom," I began, *Friday the 13th, Part 5* just came out. Is it okay if we take Mamo to it to get us in?"

"Is that the one with the guy killing everybody?"

"Yeah, Jason. The one with the hockey mask," Joaquin replied.

Mom shrugged. She would just nod as Joaquin and I

rented slasher film after slasher film at the video store, giggling at some teenager getting impaled onto a wall, bug-eyed in agony. Other parents were more restrictive, but Mom had her own system. There was a lot of latitude as long as we showed respect, behaved responsibly, and brought home good grades.

At age eleven, my brother and I essentially had no curfew. Mom was also lax about household chores. Perhaps seeing her mom cleaning and cooking for other people for so long had stigmatized certain tasks. Whatever the reason, she didn't make us do them. There weren't even hard-and-fast rules about whether we had dessert before or after dinner. Sometimes dessert was the meal.

Since moving, Mom made it a habit at large family gatherings to include us in conversations that adults were having. At Panchito's, when we'd hang out with her coworkers, she'd ask my brother and me what we thought about a municipal policy or a new volunteer project she was starting with the city.

I don't remember Mom ever shutting a door in my face, cupping her hand over the mouthpiece of a phone, or shooing me out of the room to finish a conversation. Her determination to treat Joaquin and me as intelligent young men was another form of activism born of repression. The household she'd grown up in was stifling, and she wanted her boys to grow up without their wings being clipped.

The message that Joaquin and I could talk to her about *anything* was a conscious tactic on her part. She included us in raw conversations about civil rights, and when there was news that shocked us — the assassination attempt on President

Ronald Reagan or the *Challenger* disaster, for example—
Mom made sure the three of us talked through it.

In 1985, my brother and I transferred to St. Mary's Catholic
School for fifth grade. The transition was a headache. Literally.

St. Mary's was essentially an antique cinder-block box. The
lack of windows gave it the feel of a medieval prison, updated
with weak fluorescent lighting. The odors of butter and syrup
filled the basement cafeteria and wafted throughout the school
in varying degrees of pungency.

After the first month, I was sitting in class when my head
began to feel like a balloon expanding but unable to pop. Joaquin was fine, but I was reacting to something in that school
atmosphere, and the physical pressure was too much. The pain
would fade slightly after school, but when I got home I would
drop my bag and then myself onto the bed and sleep most of
the afternoon. The next morning, I would feel better, but back
at school the swelling pressure would return.

By Christmas break, I was popping two Tylenols a day,
sometimes three, to ease the pain. I knew Mom wanted us to
finish school at St. Mary's, but I was physically struggling.

Then, early one Saturday morning, Joaquin and I stood outside the locked school waiting for basketball practice to start.
The rest of the team hadn't arrived yet. As we leaned against
the door, a squat Latino with salt-and-pepper hair and a windbreaker approached us.

"¿Qué están haciendo aquí?" He asked us what we were
doing there.

Nobody had ever treated us as though we looked suspicious,

and we were clearly in basketball uniforms waiting for the gym to open.

"Just waiting," I answered him in English.

He didn't seem to understand. I switched to Spanish. *"Somos estudiantes aquí."* We're students here, I told him.

The man took out his wallet, unfolded it, and flashed a badge, first at Joaquin and then at me.

"Necesitan venir conmigo." He wanted us to go with him.

Joaquin and I looked at each other. We weren't doing anything wrong, and Mom had raised us to stand up for ourselves and not be pushed around.

The man became impatient and raised his voice. *"¡Vámonos!"* he insisted, demanding we leave with him.

I shook my head.

"Necesitamos quedarnos aquí." Joaquin told him we needed to stay put.

The man's badge seemed suspicious, as did his dirty windbreaker and use of Spanish rather than English. We were pretty sure he wasn't a cop.

Joaquin repeated that we needed to stay there for basketball practice. My heart was racing and I thought about making a scene, but nobody else was around. Morning mass at St. Mary's Church, across the street from the school, hadn't begun, and no one was walking on the sidewalk or waiting at the bus stop nearby.

The man fixed his eyes on me. Now he was annoyed, and he gestured for Joaquin and me to go with him. I reared away, then grabbed Joaquin's arm and pulled him away from the man. Visibly frustrated, the man looked around. It was clear that my brother and I were going to put up a fight, and there was no way the man could corral both of us. He stared back at us, looked around the street again, stuck his wallet into his pocket, and quickly walked away.

After that, we mounted a campaign to get out of St. Mary's School. Although we loved Mom and wanted to please her, we were clearly not happy there. To convince Mom to put us back in public school, Joaquin and I participated in our first activist campaign. We started to bombard Mom during meals and commercial breaks. "All our friends are going to Rhodes next year," Joaquin would begin.

"We just want to be with our friends!" I'd plead and start to lay it on thick. "St. Mary's sucks. It's going to kill me. I take pills every day just to make it through the day at that place. I feel like a zombie!"

Mom had taught us well, and she was true to her principles too. She thoughtfully listened to our arguments, never pulling the Mom card. Eventually, she relented in late spring. While our arguments were persuasive, I've come to realize that Mom's decision to put us back in public school was based more on her inability to afford the tuition at St. Mary's.

During the school year, Joaquin and I had grown close to Mr. Palmerin, who was our favorite teacher. He was good at relating to students and making them laugh. He'd even offered to take Joaquin and me to see *Enemy Mine,* a science fiction movie. We'd taken the bus on a Saturday and met him at the theater. He was the most informal of our teachers and seemed eager to go beyond the boundaries of typical teacher-student relationships. He'd talk to other teachers on our behalf and had great relationships with lots of kids. It wasn't until years later, when he was sentenced for indecency with a child, that we understood that he may have been grooming my brother and me. When we heard the news as adults, Joaquin remembered a time when he'd walked into a St. Mary's bathroom and seen Mr. Palmerin with another student who was in his underwear and in the process of getting dressed. Joaquin had believed the teacher's explanation of searching the student for something illicit and didn't think anything of it until hearing the news.

I'm not sure who the patron saint of headaches is, but he or she was in my corner.

"Que Dios los bendiga," Mamo said to us and made the sign of the cross as Mom, Joaquin, and I left the house for sixth-grade orientation. The late August San Antonio heat was still broiling as we walked the five blocks to Rhodes Middle School. But there were no more headaches.

A smiling male teacher ushered us into an auditorium filled with hundreds of students and their parents. We threaded past a table and picked up class schedules, lists of school rules and expectations, lunch aid forms, and other papers.

The staff introduced themselves one by one, and after a few speeches about what to expect at Rhodes, one administrator walked up to the mic to wrap it up.

"I'm here to give every student some advice," he said in a stern voice. "I want y'all to look around the room; look at the person beside you." He waited for everybody to look around. "Statistically the chances are that up to half of you won't be here when it's time to graduate from eighth grade. That's what we're dealing with here."

Mom straightened up. Joaquin and I recognized this alertness, and it meant one thing: Mom was angry. I'd done well at St. Mary's, almost all As, except for an F in music, which Mr. Palmerin had gotten the music teacher to change to a B.

What the administrator was saying made no sense to us. Every kid we knew stayed in school, and we just assumed that they would graduate. Mom had a master's degree and Dad was a math teacher.

When the talk was over, Joaquin and I saw some buddies and walked over to them while Mom waited patiently for us at the back of the auditorium. Our friends gathered and began talking. Seven classrooms instead of one! My own locker and football and girls! Rhodes is going to be so cool, we all agreed.

Mom, however, did not agree. "You're not going to Rhodes," she announced the next morning. She didn't tell us why at the time, which was not her usual style, but years later she shared her reason with us. "I knew what you two could accomplish, and there was no way I was going to put you in a school where they set such low expectations."

Not knowing her reason at the time, however, Joaquin and I burst into arguments about friends and football and finally being able to go to a normal school. "You're going to Tafolla Middle School," Mom said. "It's a foreign-language magnet school two miles away."

Foreign-language magnet school? Joaquin and I were not even fluent in reading and writing in Spanish.

Tafolla, a two-story, rectangular brown brick building, sat across the street from the Alazan-Apache public housing project, a cluster of orange-beige brick apartment homes intersected by narrow streets and alleys. Built in 1939, the project was the first public housing complex in San Antonio, and it became home to nearly ten thousand mostly Mexican American and black tenants.

Shortly after we started sixth grade, and just as Joaquin and I turned twelve, we moved from Hidalgo Street into another two-bedroom rental house, this one on Globe Avenue, about five miles from our new school.

The new house was our first in a neighborhood where lawns were regularly mowed and hedges trimmed. The fire-engine-red paint on our house wasn't even peeling. Joaquin and I walked around the neighborhood and waved to a Mexican American man wearing jeans and a white T-shirt, who was washing his car's tires. In our previous two neighborhoods, packs of stray dogs would roam in the early morning hours, peeing on car tires.

The new house was only a little bit bigger than the ones before. Mom had her own bedroom, while Joaquin and I shared a room with Mamo. But what really made us feel rich was setting up the basketball hoop we got as a Christmas gift. At least five neighborhood kids quickly found their way over, and we had a solid group of kids playing ball.

There must have been some other issues Mom wrestled with before relocating, because she never drank again after settling in. I can't be sure whether the move was related to her decision to quit drinking, but that was how I marked the difference. I never spoke with Mom about it, but seeing her repeatedly intoxicated had been a troubling part of my childhood. I think she realized that, and I always saw it as a measure of how great her love was for Joaquin and me that she was willing to stop. Drinking had been one way for Mom to relieve some of the overwhelming pressure, but she was somehow able to give that up for her kids.

Tafolla was a magnet school, which meant students not zoned for the district could still study there. The San Antonio Independent School District bus snaked through neighborhoods, picking up kids who wanted to study Latin, Spanish, German, French, or Japanese as a second language. The halls were full of eager and intellectually curious kids, and the way the teachers interacted with us created a much more supportive atmosphere than Rhodes.

It was exciting to run our fingers down the list of language offerings. Joaquin decided to take German, for some reason I've never figured out; Japanese was the choice for me, given my love of ninjas, martial arts movies, and karate. The easy one would have been Spanish, but Mom assumed we were learning enough of that at home when we spoke with Mamo.

Tafolla was relaxed in a way that St. Mary's wasn't. Many of the teachers helped me exceed my own expectations, and I made the honor roll with my first report card. But an even more telling moment was when a teacher handed me a vihuela, the small, guitarlike instrument played by Mexican mariachis.

I shook my head. The only F I had ever received was in music class. Some people fear snakes and spiders, but for me it was musical instruments.

"I'm not good with music," I told him.

"So, are you more scared of failing or learning to do something that doesn't come very easily?"

He smiled, nodding to himself and patting the vihuela. "Have you seen one of these?"

I nodded. The instrument was a mainstay of our culture. That fact made it interesting to me, and when the teacher saw my attention lift, he put the vihuela into my arms. Although I would never become particularly good at playing the instrument, in three weeks I was gamely strumming away and enthusiastically singing mariachi classics like "Guadalajara," "El Rey," "El Carretero," and "Perfidia."

Sports were much more important to me. I'd come home with a registration sheet for basketball and football, and Mom was always encouraging (the exception was football, which she did not approve of but still allowed me to play). We now had a car—a used gold Chrysler LeBaron, which Mom was able to afford, thanks to promotions at work—and we were now mobile enough to get to and from practice easily.

At Tafolla I enjoyed my Japanese language classes. The pronunciation seemed close enough to Spanish that I was able to learn to speak basic Japanese, though the written language was quite a bit more challenging. Picking up a new language demanded a different, more serious structure, one that I thrived on. Another Mexican American kid, who wore big, Buddy Holly–style glasses, was pretty good at Japanese too. I'd never talked to him before school even though he lived in our neighborhood, but I walked over to him when we needed a partner to practice Japanese in class.

"You want to practice together?" I asked.

"Yes," he said and blurted out a line of Japanese that I answered.

Besides sharpening our language skills, we discovered a shared love of slasher films and Nintendo.

I told Joaquin about him as we took the bus home. "He doesn't live too far from us...man, I can't remember his name now."

"That kid with the glasses?" he said. "The Nerd?"

In the brutally affectionate world of childhood nicknames, when a descriptive term definitively sums up a person, it's often impossible to shake. Once I nodded that this was the person I was talking about, he became known as the Nerd. We tried not to use the nickname in front of him, but that lasted maybe half a day. Celso Hurtado smiled and pushed his glasses up for effect, as if to say, *Who, me?*

In reality, Joaquin and I weren't much different from Celso, which is why we all became such good friends. One difference was that Celso was actually more of an extrovert. I admired how easily and casually he could talk to people. He'd pop a joke that would crack up surrounding girls and could enter a conversation as smoothly as a Michael Jackson moonwalk.

After our first year of middle school, Joaquin and I would roam around in the summer heat looking for shade and activities. We'd lean against the fence at Thomas Jefferson High School, our fingers laced through the chain links, and watch people hit balls on the tennis court. At twelve, hitting anything as hard as you can is appealing, so we bugged Mom to let us try.

A worn, scrawny guy named Larry Hart gave free tennis lessons there to neighborhood kids. We didn't have racquets, but Joaquin and I walked onto the court anyway as Larry collected balls and dumped them into the dented Lobster tennis ball machine he'd unloaded from his truck.

"Hello," he said and walked over. Joaquin and I shook hands with him, which seemed to impress him.

"Polite kids," he said. "You ever played tennis before?"

We shook our heads.

"I have an extra racquet that you guys can share, but if you like it you might want to get your own."

Joaquin and I took turns as Larry fed us balls and gave us pointers. Two days later we showed up just as Larry was driving across the field to reach the court. That was one of our favorite parts of Larry's unofficial tennis camp: his disregard for school rules in a funny, friendly way. I guess he didn't want to haul his gear from the parking lot, but there was something affectionate about his grizzled manner as he off-roaded to the tennis court in his beat-up Ford pickup truck. Maybe it was his version of jumping fences.

Six weeks into summer, Joaquin and I were hitting balls almost every day. Tennis was the one sport that we were actually better at than most other kids. Our tennis *skills*, that is. Larry stopped noting our good manners when I threw my racquet toward Joaquin and dented it after he beat me on a debatable line call.

Up to that point we had behaved well, but now that we were more at ease on the court and with Larry, our competitive nature surfaced, this time with more fireworks than ever.

Because tennis is a game with very clear rules and scoring, it is hard to dispute who wins and who loses, and if you're out of position or make a poor shot, you tend to beat yourself up afterward.

That said, my brother and I could not stop gloating over wins. Once, I beat Joaquin badly enough that I just couldn't help but gloat as Larry tasked us with picking up loose balls.

"Wow, sure are a lot more on your side of the net," I said. "Have a hard time getting it over today?"

He proved he could get it over the net as he tried to bean me in the head. I retaliated.

"Castros! Stop making more of a mess!" Larry barked.

"Pick the balls up yourself," Joaquin said as he walked off the court.

"Joaquin!" Larry yelled.

"Julián said he'd pick up all the balls," he said. "He feels sorry for cheating."

Larry wasn't biting. "Pick up the balls."

The next week, Larry witnessed a repeat performance, except it might have been me who lost and moped and threw my racquet over the fence with Joaquin grinning.

Our competition at tennis was a parental tightrope for Mom, but fortunately, she knew just how to handle our rivalry. When she watched us play tennis, she always complimented both of us, no matter how much each would suck up to her and try to get her on his side.

I remember one day, when Joaquin destroyed me on the court.

"Julián," she said after we got into the car, "I love how you were down and really dug in and found a way to hang in there and come back and almost tie it."

"Yeah, but that was just once. Did you see me win?" Joaquin asked.

"Yes, I did, just like I saw your brother win last week."

Mom knew how to raise twins.

Chapter Five

Seventh grade started with a loosely organized caper. Our new life science teacher had excused herself from the classroom and told us to behave for five minutes. Three minutes in, I was bored and tapping on the glass of the fish tank when a classmate brought over a bottle of Elmer's glue.

I checked the door and saw that it was still clear as my friend and I crowded around.

"Make sure she doesn't come back," I said to the guy closest to the hallway door. "Let us know if she's coming."

I squeezed the bottle over the water, watching in fascination as the white blob stretched out and broke away, releasing the glue bomb. It seemed to sink in slow motion.

All the kids surrounding the tank laughed, which of course made me squeeze out a longer, thicker blob as I held the glue bottle higher. I circled the bottle gently to make a swirl pattern as it hit the water.

"Will the fish be glued together?" one kid asked.

I thought I was being funny, but now nobody was laughing. I looked up and saw our lookout standing with all the other kids, who seemed keenly interested in how their shoelaces were tied.

The fish were not pleased, twitching nervously away from the white strings of glue descending into their world. The teacher was also not impressed. I was about to learn how the expression "Your mother will be called, and you will see the principal tomorrow" could be conveyed simply with a stern, dissatisfied glance.

Had this happened when Dad was still living with us, he probably would have spanked me as soon as I got home. But Mom handled it differently. She didn't even raise her voice when the call came in; instead, she merely knocked a Kool out of the pack and lit it as she agreed to come in the next day and hung up the phone.

She exhaled and looked at me.

"Okay, Julián, you want to explain?"

I did not, and remained silent.

This did not mean that I was off the hook. Rather than spank me, she let me marinate all night in worry.

The next morning, I yearned for the usual boring bus ride and cursed the extravagance that enabled Mom to own a car. That fifteen-minute drive was one long, painful descent into anxiety.

"Just tell them you grounded me for a week," I pleaded. "That you took care of it."

"That would be lying. Now you want me to lie for you?"

I knew I was in deep when Joaquin didn't even use the opportunity to taunt me.

"I don't know what squirting glue into a fish tank does," Mom said. "Maybe you hurt the fish?"

I leaned back into the seat, wishing it would just engulf me and end it all.

Mom let me stress out as I sat in the back seat, walked with her into school, and sat down in the vice principal's office. She and the vice principal made agonizing small talk until Mom brought up the subject we were there to discuss.

"Julián told me what he did."

The vice principal shuffled some papers, presumably looking at my grades. He looked up at me almost out of curiosity, since this was my first offense.

"Anything you'd like to say, Julián?"

"Sorry?"

He nodded. "Two days in the alternative center."

Mom thanked him for handling the situation and waited until I shook hands with the vice principal.

She never said another word to me about it, but she taught me a valuable parenting lesson that day: when you make a poor decision, you deal with the consequences. She had seen family and friends make poor decisions in life—and she had made mistakes of her own—without thinking of the consequences, and figured this lesson would stick with me.

Mom was teaching us to navigate the real world, and did not try to create a false sense of security for my brother and me. We knew she loved us and had our backs, but she often said, "Decisions in life have real consequences," and she wasn't going to allow us the fantasy that we wouldn't have to answer for them. All she demanded, at that point and once we became teenagers, was that we be open with her.

One night at dinner, she simply said, "You can tell me whatever you want, and I'm not going to get mad at you for it. I want to know what is happening, so just don't lie to me."

She also forced us to think in a way that encouraged personal responsibility. A typical talk often turned into a thriving debate, with Mom taking a side and making us explain the reasoning behind our stance. Any topic was fair game to be employed as a tool for this teaching method.

"The Eagles are a way better football team," I'd say to Joaquin.

"Cowboys," he'd reply.

The debate would devolve into a heated quarrel until Mom butted in and made us use facts. We were free to have our own opinions—we had just better be able to back them up.

An argument about football was treated just as seriously as when Joaquin asked Mom why some of his classmates' older siblings were dropping out and why so many of our peers didn't take school as seriously as he thought they should. Our whole lives we'd heard Mamo complain about being ripped out of school, and here were kids seemingly throwing away the opportunity.

"How do you know that they realize they're throwing it away?" Mom asked.

"Because I see them messing around and not caring, or even talking about how they can't wait to get older and quit school."

"And how do you think they learned that attitude?"

That led to a discussion about family support and positive influences.

"Maybe they don't have the support you have," Mom said. "Not everybody has what you have.

"Your grandmother takes care of you," she continued,

exhaling cigarette smoke, "and I work for a car and this house, and your job is to go to school and to do the very best you can."

Joaquin and I nodded. Nobody had claimed the housecleaning job, and I looked around at the careening columns of Mamo's romance novels in the corner, the stack of laundry heaped on a chair and waiting to be folded, and the ashtray spilling over as Mom butted out a Kool. The room Joaquin and I shared with Mamo was a blast zone of clothes, wrestling magazines, football and baseball cards, and action figures.

When it came to homework, though, Mom was a tough boss. Every day, when we got home from school, we had to finish it first before playing or going outside.

Mamo's steady drinking and refusal to take her diabetes medicine and adjust her diet worried my mom. The one thing Mamo would do in a pinch was take insulin, but the dosage was never right because her lack of self-care made the insulin affect her in unpredictable ways.

One day, I came home from school by myself, put my bag on the sofa, and said hi to Mamo. She looked at me blankly at first, then seemed to snap out of it.

"Mamo? Are you all right?" I asked.

She slurred some words in Spanish that I couldn't understand. I walked over to her and held her hand, but she pulled it back.

"Mamo?"

She looked at me, confused.

I called Mom. She called Mamo's doctor, who diagnosed the problem as an insulin imbalance. "Just try to keep her comfortable and wait for the body to rid itself of some of the insulin, and she'll balance out and return to knowing who you are and who she is," the doctor said.

Mamo's insulin levels did balance out, but that incident initiated Joaquin and me into her medical care. We loved her so much, and she was such a big part of our lives, that this new awareness of her fragility scared us. Mamo was still tough enough to be alone for hours, but we all began asking her constantly if she'd eaten or checked her insulin levels lately.

Mom tried to regulate Mamo's insulin as much as possible, but she could only do so much when she wasn't home. Besides work, she had begun volunteering at Visitation House, a shelter for women and children fleeing abusive relationships. The shelter itself was too intense of an environment for us, so Mom limited our exposure to conversations at the dinner table.

The work upset her in ways we'd never witnessed before. One meal was unusually quiet until she couldn't hold back any longer. "There was this lady today at the House," she began. "We had to stop her husband from trying to kick the door in, pounding on it and demanding to see her until we called the cops."

"Did they get him?" Joaquin asked.

"No, he took off after we said we had called the cops. The police came and took statements, but there is nothing they can really do until he assaults her."

Mom was quiet. She looked at us and, in a stern voice, said, "You *never* hit a girl. *Never. Hit. Anyone.* Violence doesn't solve anything, and every night I go over there I see the damage it does and the scars it leaves on the inside and out. I see how it never goes away for some of those women and children."

She stared ahead for a moment and then relaxed.

"I know you two would never hit a girl," she said. "It's just a nightmare for some of those victims over there, and I never want to see people go through that."

That moment made it clear that the activist bug had never left her—it just went into hibernation mode for a decade or so, until Joaquin and I demanded less of her energy and attention.

The more time Mom was gone, the more Joaquin and I learned how to support each other without a parent around. But sometimes not having her home led to otherwise avoidable situations, like us nearly killing each other.

One afternoon, I remember coming home from school worked up over something and dropping my backpack on a chair, where it slid off onto the floor, spilling the contents. Like a typical adolescent frustrated by a day when nothing was going right, I vented my anger by kicking a binder, sending it scuttling across the linoleum floor. But at least now I could relax by the TV with a soda in hand. So I went to the kitchen and opened the fridge to get a Coke.

Except there was no Coke. I slammed the door shut and saw Joaquin sitting on the sofa, watching TV. And guess what? He was drinking the last Coke.

Mamo was dozing in her chair, so I shouted in a loud whisper, "That was mine!"

He looked up and furrowed his brow. "Huh? First come, first served."

When he saw how steamed I was, he smiled and took a long, slow, refreshing sip. Like a kid in a TV commercial, he finished the drink off with a nice, drawn-out "ahhh."

I ran over and kicked his legs. Surprised at my fury, he stood up and hit me in the shoulder.

I yelled, "Asshole!"

Mamo made a snort as she jerked awake in her chair.

We both looked at her silently.

I tilted my head toward the garage. He nodded.

Our somewhat systematized fighting had no name, but at that age we gravitated toward something that might as well have been called the Infinity Death Loop of Punches.

We walked out into the dingy garage. It had rained a few days earlier, so the ground was slightly wet and muddy and our socks grew filthy after the first step. Joaquin and I didn't care as we started the Infinity Death Loop. We had a system. He quickly cocked his arm and delivered a punch square on my shoulder. I did the same to him. We continued to take turns, yelling and trying to pretend it didn't hurt.

Finally, Mamo yelled at us from inside the house, and we used this as an excuse to stop. We were often crazed with Cain and Abel anger, but we never lost all of our faculties — and never hit each other around Mom. We needed a controlled structure to stop the emotional escalation, and oddly the Infinity Death Loop worked for us. People often ask me whether, as twins, Joaquin and I shared our own language. We didn't, but this was our oddball ritual, and nobody else knew about it. I hit my brother as hard as I could, and he hit me right back, but it also turned into a bonding situation when we'd compare bruises later.

We knew each other well, but there was one time in seventh grade when Joaquin truly surprised me. As identical twins, we pushed and loved and fought and supported each other, and it was rare to be caught off guard by what the other one did.

Jennifer was a cute student on the Spanish track at Tafolla. Tall and slim with light-brown skin and shoulder-length dark hair, she was the prettiest girl in our grade, and at school I daydreamed of walking down the hall holding hands with her.

Although we didn't have any classes together, we had a few friends in common, so one day I had my best bud, Celso, pass a note to her. No response. The crush got serious enough that I told Joaquin about my feelings, and once, after school, I even looked up Jennifer's number and called her, but when her mom answered I lost my nerve and hung up.

After dinner one night, I told Mom how pretty Jennifer was, and she could tell I was in deep.

"Tell her that you think she's pretty and maybe, if it's okay, the two of you could go for a walk."

"Mom," I said, laughing. "This isn't *Leave It to Beaver*. Nobody talks like that."

But I knew she was right. I finally gathered the courage to — well, to have Celso ask her if she'd "go around" with me.

Celso went off in the morning and slinked back to me later that day. His body language told me all I needed to know. Or so I thought.

"She really said, 'Who, Julián? Him? No way!'" I asked, incredulous.

"Oh, yeah, like really loud too," he said. "People laughed."

"You didn't ask her when she was alone!" I said, freaking out.

"I don't know!" Celso protested. "I've never done this before!"

It was all over school by the end of the day.

One morning two weeks later, just as the sharpness of the

pain was dulling, Celso rushed up to me and exclaimed, "Jennifer is going around with Joaquin!"

What? This was my identical twin—wouldn't Jennifer's harsh rebuff theoretically put him out of the running as well? Was I *that* different?

It turned out that my brother had learned from my mistake. I hadn't had the guts to approach her myself, so he took a more direct, and strategic, approach.

Celso filled me in. "He went up to her and made a proposal," he said. " 'Try me for a week and then you can decide if you want to keep going around.' "

She did. Then dumped him.

When I found this out, it was *almost* worth getting rejected by Jennifer. My rejection was painful, but Joaquin's was painful *and* funny. But it also showed how adept he was at reading the situation and learning from my failure. He found a way to get Jennifer to consider him differently, and it was actually pretty clever, not to mention effective.

That said, for at least a decade afterward, Celso and I would tease Joaquin at opportune times with the phrase, "Try me for a week."

Chapter Six

The sun was just coming up as Joaquin and I waited for the bus on the corner, barely awake but excited about attending high school. When the bus came we got on, slumped into our seats, and looked out the window for twenty minutes, then transferred to another bus and rode that one for twenty minutes. It was only our first day, and the morning commute had already gotten old.

Joaquin and I really enjoyed learning new languages, but that wasn't enough to outweigh the less enticing aspects of the new school. We were just about to turn fifteen, and waking up for the forty-minute bus ride was nearly a deal breaker on its own. Even if we did homework on the way home, the trip killed so much of our morning that we started complaining almost immediately. Not to mention that our best friend, Celso, was going to the neighborhood school, Jefferson High.

We didn't even last four days. It was time for a sit-down,

this time directed by Joaquin and me. Mom, true to her parenting philosophy, listened as Joaquin started the conversation.

"First off, the bus ride is way too long," he said. "We'll be getting more homework, and with over an hour spent on the bus every day, it's just too much. We want to keep playing tennis and have time with our friends still, and almost eight hours a week we'll be on a bus. That's a full work or school day just traveling."

"Celso isn't even going," I said.

Mom really liked Celso and encouraged our friendship, but we had to build a decent case to present to her.

By this point, Mom was probably getting a reputation at the school district office. She had filled out paperwork for two transfers before high school. We had started high school across town and by the end of the week were walking into another one with our best buddy, the Nerd.

Jefferson was in northwest San Antonio and could not look less like a traditional high school. Built in a Moorish design to reflect the proximity of the Old Spanish Trail, it reminded me of a mash-up of the older schools like in the movie *Grease* and an old Catholic mission built on El Camino Real in the 1700s. The main building has a silver dome influenced by Thomas Jefferson's Monticello, carved columns in the entryway, wrought-iron balconies, a Spanish-tile roof, and two large patios in the center.

Constructed during the Depression for more than a million dollars, it was one of the most expensive high schools ever built up to that point. The thirty-acre campus had baseball and football fields, a track, and tennis courts and was home to the Lasso and Wranglers Dance and Rope Team. The place was so quintessentially Texas that the building was used as a set for the 1940 movie *High School,* about a ranch girl sent to school.

Historically, Jefferson had educated the children of the doctors and lawyers who lived in the neighborhood. But over the previous few decades, the demographics had drastically changed. Many of the neighborhoods the school served had become rough, and gangs had moved in. By the time Joaquin and I walked onto campus in the fall of 1989, about 85 percent of the 2,200 students were Mexican Americans, mostly from working- or middle-class families, and the focus on learning was weak for a significant portion of the student body.

Two months in, a friend of ours from Globe Avenue who was a junior at the school offered to give us a ride home in his beat-up 1970-something Dodge. Joaquin sat shotgun and I slid into the back seat. Suddenly there was shouting, and before I was able to look out the window, our friend yelled, "Get down!" We heard a popping noise, the kind that seems more like firecrackers than gunfire. Then we heard the roar of another car's engine and the screech of tires as the driver sped away. When I finally picked my head up, I saw people running across the street and away from the car that had been shot at. Nobody got hurt, but Joaquin and I looked at each other. The forty-minute bus ride didn't seem so bad right then.

Luckily, the school tennis courts were essentially a gang-free zone. We still took tennis lessons from Larry, so we decided to try out for the school's tennis team. The afternoon temperature was already in the eighties as Joaquin and I walked onto the courts behind Jefferson's main building. Jefferson's courts had cracks that were large enough not only to affect ball bounces but even to trip over if you hit them at the right angle. The nets sagged like old clotheslines, far below regulation height. Puddles filled the depressions in the court for days after a heavy rain.

Invisible to most of the school population, Joaquin and I found an escape on the tennis court. Our coach, Ms. Gallardo, taught health, and she used that knowledge to push us physically and mentally. Brutal heat and humidity were tools to maximize our concentration and focus as we sweated through multiple shirts and wrung out our clothes afterward.

We had a special friendship with Ms. Gallardo. She intuitively knew how to push us, but that took some time because we didn't always make it easy for her. She was surprised by how we overreacted when one of us lost to the other. We could handle winning and losing against other people, but there was almost always an emotional outburst when we played together. Joaquin and I started with a clean slate and took exactly one match to get on her bad side.

That first practice, she played Joaquin against me in front of other people, and when I lost, I smashed my racquet on the ground so hard I thought I'd broken it.

"Julián! Not on my court! Pick up the balls."

I answered by throwing my racquet across the court at my bag by the fence.

Ms. Gallardo was an astute observer and quickly noticed that Joaquin and I did well in school, stayed together in the hallways and after school, and generally seemed like best friends. We were only prone to temper tantrums when pitted against each other, so she made us volley with other teammates instead, and that allowed us to laugh and learn from our mistakes.

She was also the first to team us up on the same side. She channeled our competitive natures into one force by partnering us up for doubles.

Of course, that didn't solve all of our Cain and Abel issues. We both became masters of the loud sigh of disappointment when the other messed up or missed a shot. If our team was losing badly, the game often crashed and burned in a fiery explosion of barbs and insults. But, when we won together, it was unparalleled. Our lives up until that point had many instances of zero-sum games—a major victory for one of us was a disastrous loss for the other. It was strange to have gone so long in life without sharing a victory with my best friend.

Tennis helped teach us how to enjoy things together and how to excel without anxiety. We'd spend hours practicing tennis after school and on the weekends, often just the two of us on the court, but we'd only volley against each other or practice serves, almost never keeping score.

Ms. Gallardo would bring the hammer down hard when we acted up, but she also was encouraging and pushed us harder than any coach had before. My brother and I may have appeared identical, but Ms. Gallardo understood how we needed different instruction. My backhand required different adjustments from my brother's. He was better at getting into a split step and preparing for a return. Ms. Gallardo's approach brought out the best in Joaquin and me. When I hit a wild ball out of bounds, she wouldn't just holler about losing control, she'd shout, "Julián, I know you can do better than that! Slow down and think about what you're doing. You're smart! Figure out a strategy to win."

I could handle her yelling because it was backed by a

certain confidence in me, which made me listen and process the lesson without automatically flipping into defensive mode.

As much as we liked our friends and our time on the tennis team at Jefferson, Joaquin and I were in a hurry to graduate and get on to college.

One night we were doing homework together, and I finished my last page of geometry sitting on my bed. "I wonder what Jefferson's rate of college acceptance is?" I said.

"Graduation is based on credits, right?" Joaquin replied. "We could rack up credits at summer school and night school—"

"—and skip our last year," I finished.

At first we looked at this as more of a challenge than a long-term plan. The possibility was exciting, and it allowed our competitiveness to be focused on one thing together rather than at each other. We wanted to move on to the next level of life sooner, and we both had such good grades that we didn't even think about running it past Mom—we knew she wasn't going to be against it.

Two nights later we were huddled around our desk, reading a school district pamphlet about night school. Mamo's tele-novela was blaring through the walls as we looked for the spring semester offerings. It would be a packed schedule, both day and night, but the payoff would be more than worth it.

"I feel like we are just starting to dig through a wall, tunnel-ing out of a prison," Joaquin said.

I nodded. Joaquin looked at my circled classes.

"How many classes would we need to take?" he wondered. "Which classes look good?"

"Let's check the health classes and credits," I said. We started circling potential courses in the pamphlet and cross-referencing them with other possibilities.

We never fought about which classes to take, and our bond grew tighter than ever because of our secret mission. We hadn't asked any adult for guidance. We didn't even discuss our master plan with Mom.

There were other concerns as well. Mamo was seventy-five, and her refusal to monitor her diabetes had complicated her health to the point where she was sleeping much more than usual.

One day I came home alone from tennis around four in the afternoon and dumped my backpack on the sofa.

"Mamo!" I shouted like I did every day I came home. She was planted in her regular spot, sitting on an old brown couch in the living room. She didn't stir and smile awake like she had for so many years. She hadn't even bothered to get changed out of her stained and frayed nightgown. If Mamo had one point of pride about her appearance, it was her hair, and it clung unwashed to the side of her face.

"Mamo?" She had the TV on, and for some reason my fifteen-year-old brain interpreted that to mean she couldn't be dead. "Mamo!" I shouted, and she stirred. I sat down beside her. *"¿Qué estás haciendo?"* I asked her. What's wrong? She looked up to answer me, her eyes red from crying and her lips folded inside her mouth, the way they always were when she was upset.

"Nada," she said and handed me a wrinkled white paper the size of a Post-It note. She'd scribbled "Sorry" and "Love you" on it.

"What's this?" I asked her.

"I don't want to live anymore," she said, her eyes filling with tears. "I've taken pills."

"What kind?" I asked. I'd seen her get doped up and lost when her insulin dosage was off, so I could only imagine what a few months' worth of nitro pills for her heart or blood thinners could do.

"I took these," she said and shook an empty bottle beside her. "Maybe six."

I picked up the bottle. It was extra-strength Tylenol. She'd be pain free for a while, but I was pretty sure you couldn't overdose on Tylenol.

I sat with Mamo, and we talked for more than an hour about how important she was to us and Mom.

By dinner she was back to her old self, and we never told Mom what had happened—she had far too many concerns of her own at that time. Joaquin and I had a depressed grandmother on the one hand and a mom on the other whose stress threatened her health.

During our freshman year, Mom had left her job with the Hispanic Association of Colleges and Universities and continued her activism in the community. She felt she had been blacklisted from jobs in the past due to her activism, and we wondered about her future prospects for employment.

She was admired in certain segments of the community, but those were rarely the folks in charge of the decent-paying jobs. She picked up consulting contracts and provided training, conducted interviews, and did research for grant applications. She spent a year advising Mary Roman, a contemporary running for state district judge who became the first Latina in the county to hold that office.

Even though she found fulfillment in her work, the financial stress physically ground Mom down. Her hair had grown back in about a year, but now red patches showed up on her hands and arms with a white layer of dead skin cells icing the top. She had no health insurance to pay for treatment of the psoriasis, nor did she have dental insurance to pay for the care of her teeth, which began coming loose. She always made sure Joaquin and I saw a doctor or dentist whenever we needed to, since our health was the priority for her, but that level of care didn't always extend to herself.

But physical ailments couldn't dampen Mom's energy. After decades of work by Mexican American activists like the late Willie Velasquez, who'd founded Southwest Voter Registration and Education Project in San Antonio in 1974, and due to the community's population spurt, Mexican American electoral power had steadily grown, and in San Antonio it was a recognized political force. By 1991, María Antonietta Berriozábal had served five terms on the city council and decided to run for mayor. She argued that San Antonio could boost its economy by investing in people and in neglected neighborhoods. My mother jumped on board the campaign as one of María's advisers.

Joaquin and I were sixteen years old, and several days a week after school we went directly to the campaign's headquarters near downtown instead of home. We ran errands, called volunteers on the phone, and generally got thrown in and mixed up with all the main players. Mom constantly tossed us into situations and trusted that we would glean what we needed from the experience. I saw how policy was crafted and what were the motivations behind complex issues, and I saw how much of the work was based on a vision of investing in and inspiring people.

On election night, May 4, María placed first among eleven candidates, which sent her into a runoff. Mom had been talking about what the mayoral race meant for almost a year, but back then, it often sounded like political white noise to me. I wasn't emotionally attached, except that I wanted Mom and my friends at the campaign office to win.

That evening, as Mom, Joaquin, and I left the hotel where the election night party was being held, we passed a bus stop along Commerce Street downtown. At the stop, a young Latina mother with two small children by her side noticed our María for Mayor campaign T-shirts as we walked by. "Did we win tonight?" she asked.

I remember that moment even now because I could tell that she wasn't asking us whether our preferred candidate had won. She was asking whether she and her family had won. I didn't care too much for politics yet at the time, but I thought that a candidate's victory should make people feel as though they had a stake in the outcome, that they themselves had won.

In the end, María lost the runoff by five percentage points. But while she didn't win the race, her leadership pushed the community in the right direction. I have no doubt that the path to my own election as mayor eighteen years later was paved by her and by other residents of San Antonio who believed that putting resources into things like job training, educational opportunities, affordable housing, and distressed neighborhoods would bring prosperity to the city as a whole.

Mom was shocked when we sat her down and proudly announced that we had earned enough credits to skip a year of high school. She realized that her two boys had found a creative solution to a problem that demanded a lot of discipline and determination. We'd played on the same side and taken control of our lives, and Mom was pleasantly surprised. I like to think that she also felt an overwhelming sense of satisfaction and pride in seeing her boys put into practice all she had taught us. Mom later told me that this experience made her see her two sons in a different light.

Joaquin and I hardly talked to Mom about college choices. We hadn't even discussed between ourselves the prospect of attending separate colleges. By seventeen, our unique bond encapsulated much more than sibling support. It wasn't a telepathic connection, where we could sense what the other was thinking or feeling, but we knew each other better than anyone else did. We were so similar and had so much in common that being around each other always felt comfortable, no matter what we were talking about, or whether we were talking at all. We started sending away for information about colleges, and very quickly the mailbox filled up with pamphlets and brochures.

Jefferson still had one lesson to teach us. Word got around that Joaquin and I had found a way to graduate a year early. That was interesting news in itself, but with some people the conversation led to what we were going to do after graduation.

"We just sent out for info for Stanford, Berkeley—"

"*Those* schools?" was the uniform response. "You think *you* can get into them?"

"There was one senior last year who got into Harvard," I said.

"Yeah, one kid? Needle in a haystack."

Joaquin and I always found a way to end the conversation after reactions like that. We wanted to ask, Why not try? Why defeat yourself out of fear that a college might not accept you? Some people were excited for us, but others were skeptical, as though projecting their own self-doubt.

"It's weird how some people get almost angry that we want to go to a top school," Joaquin observed one day on the way home from school.

"I don't get it," I said. "Why not aim high?"

"We're definitely gonna do that," Joaquin said.

Joaquin and I knew that it was up to us to believe in ourselves and that Mom was there to help us maintain a positive outlook. Mom reinforced that sentiment, always encouraging us and never allowing us to fall back on excuses. Even before high school, we realized how blessed we were to always be pushed and felt bad for kids who didn't have a similar support system. Mom didn't insist that Joaquin or I take one particular path or another, but she did expect us to keep trying our best and reach as high as we possibly could.

We focused intently on achieving our goal, and it felt like such a unique one that we didn't have many models to follow. For example, we didn't know how to gauge our chances of being accepted by certain colleges, so we just went ahead and worked hard without knowing where it might take us. Our hard work would pay off: we both graduated near the top of our class of 388 students.

We began going to the library to search for information on how to effectively apply for college. Joaquin and I pulled out the *U.S. News & World Report*'s college rankings and applied to all the top-ten schools, plus a few universities closer to home, such as the University of Texas at Austin and Trinity University in San Antonio, as a backup. While we were enjoying the second half of our last year, we were awaiting replies from universities across the country.

By March, fat packets began hitting the mailbox. Princeton and the University of Pennsylvania accepted me, while Harvard rejected me and Notre Dame wait-listed me. Joaquin and I were both accepted at a number of other schools. The University of California at Berkeley was the first school that took us both. As we waited for other replies, we felt a sense of victory, and we knew we were California bound. But we hadn't yet heard from our real goal: Stanford.

I've been known to miss a birthday or two, but Friday, April 3, 1992, is a date I'll never forget. Two identical 8½-by-11-inch white envelopes with green borders sat in our mailbox. As most college applicants know, thick packets are a thumbs-up while thin ones are usually a thumbs-down.

Like some sort of ritual, Joaquin and I walked in holding our unopened envelopes, and called out to Mom and Mamo. Then we ripped them open.

"Welcome to the Stanford Class of 1996," the letter began. As Joaquin and I took turns reading the acceptance letter, it began to sink in what that moment meant to the multiple generations sitting there in that small kitchen. Mamo, orphaned and yanked out of school by the third grade. Mom, struggling and sacrificing to teach and support us so that we could have opportunities exactly like this. These two envelopes were a collective victory, a family achievement.

I wish I'd had a cell phone camera to capture Mamo's face in that moment. She'd been deprived of a formal education and the advantages that come with it. She never could have imagined that such an opportunity would be possible.

Joaquin and I began picturing our new lives in California, mostly based on what we'd seen on TV. The Lakers were celebrities, surfing was becoming mainstream, and every detective show seemed to be based there. Joaquin had already thought about a career in law, so he was attracted to *L.A. Law,* which made the West Coast appear like some sort of paradise. Also, there were plenty of Mexican Americans in California, and its being a border state offered some sort of familiarity.

In our do-it-yourself approach to college, we hadn't considered that each school had different prices. The following week more envelopes came, and reality hit hard. It cost $27,000 per student to attend Stanford each year, including tuition, books, room and board, and various living expenses.

I looked at the paper in my hand. All this work, only to have to stay home and attend a local college because of the price? Mom had earned less than $20,000 the previous year, and now her two kids had to scrape together $54,000 for the first year of college.

Less than a week later, a financial aid package arrived, and we learned a lot more about how the system worked. It bridged the gap between our means and expenses. Of the $27,000 annual cost, the university offered to cover a little more than $20,000 in combined Pell grants and university scholarships.

Government-backed loans, a work-study program, and Mom's contribution made up the rest.

We had five months left in San Antonio.

Mom's longtime friends Choco Meza and Blandina Cardenas organized a going-away party for us, which was essentially a fundraiser. The Mezas bought us luggage, and others gave us cash and bedsheets, lamps, and other necessities for our dorm rooms. The requisite chicken salad sandwiches, tamales, and cake were served, along with a wonderful sense of pride and love for Joaquin and me.

Joaquin got a summer job at Kmart while I scored a gig at a local Pep Boys, and we worked right up until our last weekend in San Antonio. Mom, Mamo, Joaquin, and I had always been packed tight into small rental houses, and that closeness created a unique web of love, stress, complicated relationships, and constant encouragement. Joaquin and I felt supported, but we also understood that we were breaking up that bond. Even if it was with Mom and Mamo's full backing, our departure brought a faint sense of melancholy into the house.

On our final weekend, we spent the days packing and hanging out with family and friends. There was no fear or doubt in my brother's or my mind. We'd done it: shaved a year off high school and gotten into our dream school. I imagined learning to surf on the weekends as sunbathers lay on the beach near palm trees. Mamo puttered around, nervously watching us pack. I had some shorts that looked extremely bland compared to the surf trunks in the TV shows, but I figured I'd find some better ones in California. My Discman was packed with a wallet of CDs. A few books and a toiletries bag, and there was no room left as I zipped up my new American Tourister bags, like a hardened Viking off to conquer new lands.

The bags didn't fit in Mom's car. We'd never had to transport luggage in the trunk before and had just assumed it would all fit. Mom called on the nuns she knew for help. Sister Neomi Hayes, the codirector of Visitation House, where Mom had been volunteering for years, pulled up and waited in her dented old Chevrolet Chevelle. She opened a trunk that had only slightly less square footage than our home, and we loaded in all the bags. We turned to say good-bye to Mamo, who was standing on the porch. We hugged her for a long time, and I went in for a second one. Her lips started folding in, and tears welled in her eyes.

Mamo made the sign of the cross. *"Que Dios los bendiga,"* she blessed us, for what must have been the seven thousandth time in my life. As she waved from the porch, tears running down her face, she stood erect, her posture straighter than usual.

Dad and a few of our Jefferson friends met Joaquin, Mom, and me at the airport terminal. Dad had not been a consistent influence in our lives, but it meant a lot to have him there to see us off. He was proud of his two boys and had made it a point to buy our Southwest Airlines tickets to San Francisco. We hung out a bit awkwardly, none of us really knowing how to act.

We posed for pictures, and I walked over to Dad for a good-bye hug. He embraced me and then pulled back, looking me in the eye. "I love you, m'ijo," he said. "We'll talk later." That was the first time I could remember him telling me that he loved me. In his eyes and in his voice was an acknowledgment of the distance between us—the separation that was about to happen, and the one that had happened long ago.

"Okay," I said. Then I hugged Mom and nodded to Joaquin as we picked up our carry-on bags, turned, and walked toward the gate, ready to start a new life in California.

Chapter Seven

I sensed the airplane's wheels lift off the ground, and the weightlessness I felt made my stomach turn. The wheels folded up into the plane and the hatch closed, triggering a tightness in my throat as I attempted to hold back a surging tide of emotions. At least I had Joaquin sitting in the next seat, steeling me.

I looked over, and he was already staring at me, eyes wide with emotion. I watched them fill with water, and my lip started quivering. Then his lip started quivering.

We both emotionally collapsed at once, and boy, was it ugly. Hiccups, snot bubbles, sobbing. We didn't care. We didn't even know what we were crying about. We'd never spent more than a few days away from home, and we missed our family already.

Crying is hard work, but we were athletes, so we kept it up the entire fifty-five-minute flight to El Paso, our first stop. A flight attendant did a couple of passes before returning with a stack of drink napkins for us to wipe our tears away with. Dad must have bought us the cheapest tickets possible, because we flew from San Antonio to El Paso to San Diego to San Francisco. Seven hours of traveling, reminding me of those long bus rides and transfers that were the norm growing up without a car.

One of Mom's activist friends had a son at Stanford Law School, and he met us at the airport and fit all our luggage into the trunk of his car. He drove us through the hills to Palo Alto and toward the East Bay, chatting away and giving us advice and encouragement as I stared out the window, zoned in on a new reality. We spent the night at his mother's house, and in the morning he drove us to Stanford's campus.

It felt as if we had driven onto the set of a TV show. Sandstone buildings with Spanish-tile roofs and palm trees lined University Avenue, and countless students on bikes crisscrossed each other's paths in a sort of organized chaos. We stopped, and I stepped out of the car. The California sunshine was strangely cinematic, and the air felt and smelled different than in Texas, as the scent of freshly cut grass rose from manicured lawns and wafted in the breeze. Here we saw black squirrels scampering up trees, whereas we were used to seeing stray packs of dogs running through the early morning streets.

Stanford University is known as the Farm, a throwback to the days when founders Leland and Jane Stanford used the land as a horse farm—about eight thousand acres nestled between San Francisco and San Jose, in the heart of Silicon Valley. The campus had about seven hundred buildings, and a giant red *S* was planted dead center in an expansive front lawn. Seven thousand students lived on campus. Joaquin and I were excited and proud, and determined to succeed. We were starting fresh in a place where our background didn't really matter in the ways it had in San Antonio. Everybody had gotten here somehow, and we were all on a level playing field.

The undergraduate college at Stanford admits fewer than 10 percent of those who apply, and the university prides itself on being the center of technological innovation. Stanford alumni have founded many of the world's most successful tech companies. When Joaquin and I arrived, the dot-com boom that would make billionaires of grads like Google founders Sergey Brin and Larry Page was still five years off, but the university was already famous for having launched the careers of tech pioneers like Bill Hewlett and David Packard.

Joaquin and I felt very far away from home, so we wanted to live in Casa Zapata, a Chicano-themed dorm named after the leader of the Mexican Revolutionary war, Emiliano Zapata. There was a lottery system and we didn't get in; instead we were assigned different dorms on the east side of campus, across a grass field from each other. This would be the first time we had ever lived apart.

I was assigned to Soto, a freshman dorm in Wilbur Hall. As I walked up to check in with a group of college-age staffers at the reception table outside the entrance, they greeted me upon sight by shouting out, "Julián!" They pronounced it with a Spanish *J* and an emphasis on the *a*—not "JOO-lee-in," but "who-lee-AHN." All through school I'd grown up hearing the English-sounding Julian, even in Mexican American neighborhoods of San Antonio, and here in California, in a school with people from around the world, they nailed my name on the first try.

The school was immensely diverse, and you'd hear many

different languages, accents, and slang terms in the hallways or in cafeteria lines. College is fantastic for a variety of reasons, but that opportunity to bond with people of very different backgrounds, to pull knowledge — big and small — from such a diverse pool, is invaluable, especially in the formative years.

Moving into a different environment like this gave me the space to truly appreciate and exhibit pride in my own background, including in my name. From then on, I always referred to myself as Julián, never Julian. I felt in charge of my life and my future, and that confidence informed my decisions in the years to come.

After settling into our rooms, Joaquin and I explored the new living areas. In a university known for pioneering modern advances, it made sense that the campus incorporated cutting-edge technology. Every dorm had its own computer room, with Macintosh desktops and one NeXT desktop available to students. Joaquin and I walked into the computer room in my dorm. At Jefferson we had used clunky, slow PCs and had seen a Mac once in a blue moon. To us the machine looked like an intergalactic control system. Joaquin needed to set up his email account, so he sat down at a terminal and hit the keyboard. Nothing happened. He picked it up and looked to see if it was plugged in. It was, and he fumbled around hitting the Option and Control keys and just making a symphony of error beeps.

Then he saw a small white gadget tethered to the computer by a cord and sitting atop a black foam pad. We thought it was some sort of presentation aspect of the computer, and Joaquin didn't know what to do with it. He flipped it over and noticed a little plastic gray ball in the center. He rolled it with his finger.

"Oh! Look!" I said, pointing to the cursor on the computer screen.

Joaquin tried to navigate it toward the line he needed to type on, but it jerked around erratically.

"What's wrong with this thing?" he asked.

A student across the table was looking at us curiously. From a technological standpoint, we were like cavemen.

"You have to turn it over," he said. "Like this." He pointed at his mouse, sitting white side up on the black pad. We looked at him and then back at our mouse as if it were a Rubik's Cube. Ours was like a flipped turtle, rocking back and forth as we flicked the gray ball, continually tipping it to one side.

"Slide it on the pad!" another student yelled.

How to use a mouse—my first lesson at Stanford.

There is a family story that haunted me during my arrival at Stanford. One of my distant cousins had dedicated himself to getting into a prominent college, found a way to pay tuition, and left home just like we did—amid tears and well wishes, a bon voyage to a new life. Two semesters later, he returned home, shell shocked. Actually, *culture shock* was how family members described it. There was no shame, only an odd sense of pride that the student had been accepted and yet made the choice to return to a loving home environment that couldn't be found elsewhere.

During our farewell party, one of our mother's friends had said as much to me. "I'm so proud of you! But, you know, if you ever don't like it out there or can't make it, then you can return here, and we'll all be here for you." It was meant as an expression of affection, but it felt like an expression of doubt.

Still, Joaquin and I had to find a way to adapt. You either cut it at Stanford or you didn't. We had attended an overwhelmingly Mexican American high school in a majority Latino working-class community, and we'd barely left the county, never mind the state. And while there was some doubt about the quality of the academics at our school, we both knew that there were plenty of people at Jefferson who would have done well at Stanford if they had had the opportunity to go there.

We were mightily impressed by our surroundings, no question about it. A casual conversation with a classmate might hint at a superstar intellect. People were clearly smart, but I felt that if I worked hard, I could do well at Stanford. And, again, Joaquin and I had each other to lean on and prop up in times of stress.

My freshman roommate at Stanford had nobody to lean on. Hailing from a small town in the Rio Grande Valley of South Texas, he'd attended public school like me and was planning to study engineering, one of Stanford's toughest majors. He struggled and sometimes overslept. Cell phones with unlimited calling were not a reality yet, and long-distance calls were expensive, so he couldn't even find comfort by talking with old friends and family regularly.

When I needed to take a break, I would often walk over to Joaquin's dorm or invite him to come to mine. We'd catch *The Wonder Years* or a football game on TV. Having my brother and best friend so close by made a world of difference, especially our freshman year.

My roommate, meanwhile, left after freshman year and never came back to Stanford.

It made my blood boil to think about the differences in opportunity among my Stanford classmates. Joaquin and I essentially had to forge our own path to Stanford ourselves while so many classmates were essentially put on a path to Palo Alto from very early on. They were all smart, deserving students who mostly worked hard to get there, but given the disparity in economic backgrounds, nobody could look at the routes taken to Stanford and say that they were equitable.

One evening at dinner, about a week after we'd arrived, we finished some slightly stale fish and were digging into multiple scoops of ice cream. One student mentioned how easy a history AP class was at his high school compared to his current class. There were groans of agreement.

"All eight of my AP classes were mostly just extra homework," another student said.

"Eight? Lazy bastard. I took ten."

"Loafer," a third said, scooping too much chocolate ice cream into his mouth. "Whelfve."

"What?" we all said.

"Whelfve," he said, frustrated as ice cream started dripping out of his mouth. He tipped his head up, holding a finger out for pause as he swallowed.

"You make eating ice cream look hard," Eight APs said.

"Twelve!" he finally said, his mouth clear of ice cream. "I took twelve AP courses."

I was embarrassed. It wasn't my fault, but I felt self-conscious about my comparatively threadbare education. I'd taken two AP classes at Jefferson—and the school only offered three.

This inequity in our country's education system has never stopped seeming like one of our most chronic problems. It is painful to think of a kid forced to swim upstream, only to arrive at the same spot as somebody who had the opportunity placed in front of him. Sure, both kids have to achieve, but the effort and available support and resources are often incomparable. I understood, without any malice toward my friends at the table, what Mom and many others had fought for and how much further we all still had to go in this country.

Still, we'd gotten into Stanford, and now the rest was up to us. We didn't have the academic background that many of our classmates did, but we made up for that with sheer effort. I studied more than I ever had before, taking breaks with *The Wonder Years* when needed and blasting music by Counting Crows and Selena to keep my energy up as I studied into the night. Scared that I would fall behind and be unable to escape the avalanche of assignments and test prep, I built in a buffer by staying two weeks ahead of all my reading assignments. I even bought a felt marker and wrote "PREPARE PREPARE PREPARE" on a piece of paper that I taped to the wall above my desk lamp. I'd sit down and look at my mantra before studying.

Soto was a three-story co-ed dorm with a reputation for being a boring place with bad food compared to the bigger dorms and the rowhouses on campus. But in my opinion, if you stuff enough college students into a tight place, it will be anything but boring.

Heyning, one of my dorm mates, was a five-foot-five math whiz with thick glasses and a high-pitched voice. If he had been cast in a movie, he might have seemed like a stereotype of a smart student. But Heyning was all real and all genius, and he quickly became one of my favorite people to bump into late at night. He'd get stressed and find comfort pacing the hallway at night, jangling his keys like a janitor. Joaquin and I were often at each other's dorms, and we'd never pass up a chance to talk to Heyning as he paced. Not only was the guy beyond smart, but the way he thought of life and the world was refreshingly unique. One night we heard the sound of his keys and I opened my door to say hi. He nodded to us, and we started a conversation in the hallway. Joaquin was talking about a cute girl in one of his classes. Heyning shook his head.

"What?" Joaquin said. "You don't even know her!"

"No girls," he said.

"You don't like girls?" I asked. I didn't care who he liked, but I was curious that he didn't want to get involved in any relationships. We were at college, after all.

He tapped his head. "Reptilian side of the brain, the primitive part." He shook his head as if to fight its influence, as if just mentioning it called it to attention. "First to develop. If I shut that out then I can focus on my studies. It's just a distraction."

"Just a distraction?" Joaquin said and laughed.

"But it's, like, one of the best distractions!" I said.

Heyning respectfully disagreed. I wasn't going to argue with his logic — I knew what kind of grades he got.

Then, as a contrast, there was Jon. A Californian in the mold of Jeff Spicoli of *Fast Times at Ridgemont High,* he always seemed to be holding a beer in one hand and dribbling a basketball with the other. Jon was a lesson in how you can succeed and still be relaxed. After all, he wasn't smoking weed at the beach — he was at Stanford! He had that magical California nod that only a native acquires. It's a fluid, welcoming gesture that can only be interpreted as saying, "This is pretty good, isn't it?" And when you live in a place that averages seventy degrees and is sunny all the time with miles of beautiful beaches, then, yeah, just like with Heyning, I wasn't going to argue with that logic.

Dorm life was also my social life. The surrounding town, Palo Alto, was an affluent community that had some nightclubs, but going there was never something Joaquin and I felt comfortable doing. We didn't own a car or bikes, and we rarely ventured off campus. We were happy enough just hanging out with friends in a dorm lounge or at a campus party.

As inviting and casual as those gatherings were, it still took some time before I felt comfortable. I hadn't attended many high school parties, and at college we were thrust into a completely different culture. The first party I went to at Stanford had a keg, and the place was already littered with Solo cups when I arrived. I began talking to a few folks and noticed a sea of red cups bobbing around me. I continued talking but could not stop fixating on those cups, which seemed like some trendy accessory that I needed to have.

Except that I didn't drink. As a child, I had learned to keep a casual distance when Mom's friends gathered to drink—always fun and relaxed at first, but as the beer cans emptied, the atmosphere changed to one of blustery emotions, with charged bursts of hysterical laughter and occasional heated arguments. I wondered why these smart, pleasant people would do something that turned them into lesser versions of themselves. Growing up, I tried not to pass judgment when people drank, but I had no desire to do it myself.

The embarrassing part of that first Stanford party was how insecurely I reacted to my peers' drinking. My dorm mates weren't even noticing that I didn't have a drink in my hand, but I did and felt out of place. This had nothing to do with drinking and everything to do with my confidence and image of myself. I excused myself from a conversation, went over to the leaning tower of Solo cups, and took one off the top. I went to the bathroom and filled the cup with water, then spent the next two hours at the party slowly sipping tap water. I only did that once, but it made an impression on me. I realized that I would be much better off just being myself around people. That way I'd attract friends who liked the real me, not some person I was trying to be.

Then, the zits came. I guess they were technically zits, but what began emerging from my face were basically miniature volcanoes bubbling upward with so much pressure that the skin discolored into deep purple patches. I knew it was bad as I was walking out of the dorm and ran into a friend.

"Julián! You get your ass kicked?"

I looked at him questioningly as he leaned in for a closer look.

"Oh, those are . . . what are those, zits? Those are massive."

Having painful zits like bruises made me less inclined to venture into the Solo cup jungle, so I went into hermit mode until I could see a doctor back in San Antonio. The man was in his seventies and far from the picture of health one hopes to see in a doctor. When he looked at my face he nodded immediately, as if he'd been diagnosing the problem for the last fifty years, which he probably had.

"Cystic acne," he said and without missing a beat, almost with perfect comic timing, he continued: "Don't worry, it'll go away in four or five years."

Okay, no offense to older people, but the sense of time is very different for a young person when it comes to acne. Four or five years was my entire adolescence at that point, whereas it was just a fraction of time for this man. Not to mention that it was the entire time I'd be at college.

Fortunately, I managed to find my pace at Stanford and stopped stressing so hard. Life at school was all about maintaining a rhythm and not feeling overwhelmed, and I eventually found that groove. The pimples thankfully receded in a matter of months, not years.

Growing up, Joaquin and I were essentially immersed in Chicana activism. Because that had always been our worldview, as well as a force in the community around us, we had a skewed perception of how that played into the greater American sensibility.

Early on at Stanford, I was writing a paper for English class, a personal essay about my background. I was on the Macintosh, and as I typed, I noticed red squiggly lines underlining spelling mistakes. Great! I no longer needed a dictionary on my desk for reference. I finished my paper and was reviewing it, correcting the misspelled words by clicking the mouse button and deciding which correct spelling to use. I always was given the correct replacement.

Almost always.

"Chicano" was written throughout my essay, but every time it had the red squiggly line underneath. I highlighted the first instance and hit the button. Microsoft Word made a recommendation: did I really mean "Chicago"? That made me think about how relatively unknown, even invisible, the Chicano community was to the vast majority of Americans. It meant a lot to me growing up, but most people didn't even know what "Chicano" meant. And, I thought, the majority of Latinos probably don't consider themselves Chicanos.

That said, at that age I wasn't keenly aware of the discrimination that others experienced. There were few Jewish, Native American, gay, or transgender people in my childhood circle. My small group of friends from kindergarten to high school were all Mexican American, and the fight for civil rights was highly personalized in my household and area of the city.

I would not be surprised if other students heavily submerged in other ethnic cultures encountered the same sense of marginalization when they wrote their papers on the Macintosh. One of the most interesting classes I took, "Europe and the Americas," detailed the systematic and brutally efficient decimation of indigenous peoples and cultures. One of the required books,

I, Rigoberta Menchú, recounted the struggle of indigenous Guatemalans. Later on, in "Imagining the Holocaust," I heard the horrific account of what happened to Jews during World War II. At Stanford I was forced to pull back from my tight community and understand how a common thread ran through so many other cultures around the world where people had to fight for their rights. When one of these groups achieved a victory against discrimination, I felt like the mother at the bus stop who had asked if "we" had won the election.

Joaquin and I would keep an eye on cheap flights and fly home during some of the breaks. Every time we returned, it didn't feel quite the same as it had before we left for college. It's natural to notice changes in yourself when you return to your old stomping grounds. Most people think dorm life is cramped, but our room at home felt like a car trunk. It was almost too small for one person, and now it seemed ridiculous and extraordinary that my brother, Mamo, and I had slept in that space all those years. Joaquin and I couldn't even pass each other in the room without bumping. Only two feet separated Mamo's daybed and our bunk bed. Mamo had filled her closet with clothes and mementos while Joaquin and I managed to stuff our clothes into one dresser.

Mamo's health was more concerning. Of course, Mom was well aware of Mamo's issues.

"Remember when she was discharged from the hospital after we thought she had the flu?" Mom said. "She's hardly walked out of the house since. She has a hard time walking the five feet to the bathroom and back to her sofa and her bed, and it's getting worse."

I thought about how she went out to the porch to see us off to Stanford. The thought that she could barely walk out that front door these days made me sad. Mom was on her own with this, and it pains me to say it, but Mamo only made it worse by never taking medicine and ignoring almost every issue until Mom was forced to deal with it. Mom loved Mamo, but she often seemed in over her head now. As prepared and wonderful as she had been caring for Joaquin and me, Mom seemed less prepared and less able as a daughter to care for her mother. Mamo was so passive toward life that she was a tremendous responsibility for Mom.

"It hurts to say, but we may need to think about a nursing home," Mom said.

"Ugh," I said. "I've heard so many horror stories about nursing homes—all the neglect, lack of cleanliness, abuse by other residents and the staff."

We all nodded. Our reluctance was cultural too. Respect for elders within most Latino families demands that they be cared for in the home.

"We need to also think about Mamo getting the care she needs," Joaquin pointed out. "She is sick, and maybe being in a place that could regularly administer medicine would actually make her healthier."

"If it gets any more demanding..." Mom trailed off, shaking her head. "I can't do much more, and when I'm at work I'm constantly worrying."

Caring for Mamo did get much more demanding, and Mamo went in and out of the hospital as her diabetes worsened. One time, we flew home to see her, and when Mom, Joaquin, and I walked into her hospital room and said her name, there was no response. She seemed somewhat awake. I waved and waited for that trademark Mamo smile, but she was clearly struggling and confused. Then she was still, as if fighting for consciousness. We held her hand, and slowly she began to whisper, but her words made no sense. Then she dropped out of consciousness.

Mom hurried out of the room and returned with two nurses, who began treating Mamo for diabetic shock. Clearly, she could no longer live at home. We looked at nursing centers, and Mom decided on Retama Manor, where Mamo would receive constant supervision.

We were familiar with Retama Manor, which was near our old house on Hidalgo Street, across from the San Fernando Cemetery and a string of shops that sold piñatas. Its odd location lent a strange atmosphere for people visiting relatives there. Every time the three of us visited, there was a tenant parked out front, brakes locked on the wheelchair, taking long drags on a cigarette. If the piñatas weren't a dead giveaway for the area's demographics, then the soundtrack for the nursing center made it obvious. You'd walk in the front door and be assaulted by TVs blasting telenovelas, far too loud for anybody but the aged viewers in the compact living room.

Mom visited Mamo several times a week, and Joaquin and I fast became locals when we came on breaks. We never expected Mamo to fit in, but she seemed energized by her new environment. During one visit, Joaquin and I were talking to her when she stopped and pointed to a dapper old gentleman strolling down the hallway in loose-fitting clothes.

"That's the one," Mamo said and giggled. "He's dated three ladies here. He tried to talk to me, but I wasn't interested."

The three of us were amazed that Mamo not only accepted being in a nursing home but seemed to take to it. The timing of the move was right too, for she began needing more and more care on a regular basis.

Astonishingly, Mamo García moved in to the same nursing home. Mamo's guardian had truly ended up being with her for life. Although Mamo still had a complicated relationship with her, the two of them were family, and Mamo was happy to be with Mamo García again.

Chapter Eight

I knew a classmate at Stanford whose mom worked at the White House, and she suggested that students apply for a summer internship there. Joaquin and I filled out the application form and forgot about it as we continued our studies and looked into other internships over the summer. One of those was with KSAT-TV, the ABC affiliate in San Antonio. My brother and I had been thinking about a career in broadcast journalism, and we figured that eight weeks of seeing it from the inside would be invaluable and perhaps create connections for jobs after graduation.

KSAT-TV called us back, and a few days later we toured the station and met with the assignments editor. Joaquin and I imagined ourselves pursuing hard-hitting investigative pieces, helping with research, and maybe interviewing people for leads, learning from pros how to dig for stories that made positive change.

Joaquin asked the editor about these types of stories. The

editor paused, then said, "There's more of an appetite for big fires and shootings, gang violence and crimes. That's what the viewers want to see."

We spoke with the editor for another ten minutes, and almost immediately after leaving the station we began to wonder whether local TV journalism was really for us. A couple of weeks afterward, I received a letter from Washington stating that I was accepted as an intern for the Office of Cabinet Affairs. Not the sexiest title in politics or the White House, but it was a start.

Joaquin waited for his letter in the mail. Nothing. There was no logical reason why one identical twin with an essentially identical résumé would get accepted while the other was rejected. Time was running out, and after a few weeks with no White House letter, Joaquin heard back: his application had been lost somewhere along the way. Joaquin had to make other plans, so he secured an internship with a law firm in San Antonio. I scrounged what money I could and made a trip to Solo Serve, a discount clothing store in San Antonio. I needed a wardrobe for Washington, DC, so I bought two suits for work, two pairs of casual slacks, and a black jacket on sale.

This summer would be the first time we were split for any significant period. Luckily, we were used to feeling a little more independent since we lived in different dorms at Stanford and took some different classes. I really came to value that distance because it made me appreciate Joaquin as a friend as well as a sibling.

I stared out the window of the cab as we drove through Washington, and the city looked different from what I had imagined. I had only seen the monuments and areas around the White House on TV and in magazines, and I hardly knew anything else about the city. The cab pulled up to an old building, and I got out, slightly intimidated. Old buildings in Washington looked a lot different from old buildings in San Antonio. In Washington, their facades bore the serious look of American political history, not to mention twelve layers of peeling paint. Some of the areas I'd seen appeared old enough that I was sure the view hadn't changed much in a century.

I thanked the driver, lugged my baggage out of the trunk, and walked into a boarding house for Catholic social justice workers, where I'd stay for a week until moving into the Silver Spring home of Choco Meza, the friend of my mom's who'd given Joaquin and me the American Tourister luggage that I still used. A native of Eagle Pass, where Mamo had crossed the border as an orphan, Ms. Meza worked at the Department of Housing and Urban Development in the White House. She lived in Silver Spring, Maryland, and I took the train into Washington each day like a seasoned White House veteran. There were energized political operatives everywhere I went—in restaurants, waiting in line for coffee, talking in huddled groups outside bars, sitting on steps intently waving cigarettes to emphasize a point to a reporter scribbling in a notepad.

To me, Washington was the ultimate seat of power—this is where laws were written and political careers made and broken. People hustled, talked, survived, and interacted in a manner completely new to me. In the White House, staffers conducted business and themselves in a manner unlike anything I'd ever experienced. Intelligent minds from all over the country and the world were laser focused, formulating complex deals, compromising, advising, setting up meetings, and working within a labyrinthine and nuanced machine to improve people's lives.

It took me a while not to feel like a kid walking around in a White House costume. I'd get my security badge with "A" clearance scanned before making the quick walk across the black-and-white tiles into the Eisenhower Executive Office Building directly across from the West Wing. The West Wing! That was the end of my imaginary participation in the world of power politics, for the office I worked in looked like a glorified closet. But I still saw my internship as a way to have a seat at the establishment table for the first time. Yes, I was an intern and didn't do anything of tremendous importance, so it was more like a seat at the kiddie table, but it still counted to me.

My workday ran from nine to five-thirty, during which time I answered phones, took notes in meetings, sent emails, and did other mundane tasks that required only the most generic form of participation. The experience, of course, was invaluable and gave me a useful sense of the political world at the highest level. I was inspired by the demanding and complicated nature of the work being done around me, the people who dedicated their lives to causes they were passionate about, and the special kind of joy that resulted when a hard-fought policy proposal became law.

Washington was the base of an establishment that my family never belonged to and felt very distant from. Yet while the setting was completely different, the energy was very similar to what I had sensed watching Mom and her friends organize rallies around beers at the kitchen table. I realized during that summer how important it is to have people working both on the inside and on the outside to make progress.

Luis Fraga had joined the Stanford faculty in 1991, the year before Joaquin and I arrived. A native Texan and Mexican American, he studied at Harvard and Rice University before accepting the associate professor position in the political science department at Stanford. His courses focused on the impact of minority voting on the democratic process, particularly in urban communities. In 1995, our third year at Stanford, Joaquin and I shuffled in and sat down in his class, "Urban Politics and Policy," where he spent more than an hour passionately breaking down discriminatory election structures. Never before had a class aligned so completely with my life experiences.

Luis believed that minority elected officials could and should represent both their own communities and the larger community effectively. "So you have a policy that is obviously good for one group," he would say, "but how do you articulate and convey that message to multiple groups in a way that would appeal to their own self-interest?"

Joaquin and I were familiar with the perspective of those fighting for the rights of one marginalized group. Luis was showing us that although that fight was worthy, it was vital to think about how *everybody* had to contribute so that we all could progress past the point of disenfranchisement.

"That's informed public interest," he said. "Candidates, especially minority candidates, are best served by appealing to an informed public interest. We all win that way."

Joaquin and I felt instantly comfortable around Luis. He seemed like an academic version of the people Mom always had around her at meetings, social gatherings, and work projects. Luis recognized how deep our roots were in living what he taught about, and we developed a friendship with him.

One day, the three of us were talking about Mom's early campaign. "Let's go into my office," he said and started to pack up his books after class. Joaquin and I followed, and we all sat down.

"So," Luis said, "what is it you guys want to do down the line?"

"Umm...law, maybe," I said. "I interned at the White House." I'd never been in a conversation like this with a professor before.

"Maybe journalism," Joaquin said, learning already from my unsure response. "I interned at a law firm, but I still have an interest in journalism."

He looked at us and nodded. "Tell me about what your mom did in San Antonio," he said. "Were you guys very interested or involved?"

We spoke in a much more conversational manner for almost an hour, and Joaquin and I left his office feeling like we'd just made it past the velvet rope.

One of the great things Luis did was pull Joaquin and me into his academic world and make us feel that we were contributing to his learning as well. He taught us by making Joaquin and me part of the process. He never sat us down and told us how and what to do; instead, he made us roll up our sleeves and get in there with him.

My mother at her
senior prom, 1965

My parents, Rosie Castro and Jesse Guzmán

1971 campaign poster for the
Committee for Barrio Betterment

Joaquin and me (left) in
our childhood home

At seventeen months old
under Mamo's watchful
eye

Joaquin and me (right)
at home, 1977

Jesse Guzmán,
mid-1980s

Joaquin and me (right) with Mamo on our twelfth birthday

Joaquin and me (right) at our graduation from Stanford in 1996

Celebrating victory with Erica and Carina on Election Night, 2009

Opening up Café College

Campaigning for Pre-K 4 SA with Joaquin (right)

On the White House lawn with the family

Giving Cristián a tour of my
HUD office

Meeting the Pope *(Official
White House Photo by
Pete Souza)*

With Erica at our wedding, 2007

Carina and me at
Disneyland, 2013

One day, he approached us with an idea. "I've been working on a book about the effect that Dallas and San Antonio's single-member-district electoral systems has had on minority representation. Would you two like to assist in research?"

It felt so natural that we didn't even have to think about it before we agreed.

The summer of 1995, we returned home ready to carry out the precise but laborious task that Luis had requested. Part of his research involved examining the beginnings of established discrimination in the electoral process in San Antonio. In the 1950s, a group of business leaders and other professionals from the city's white upper-class neighborhoods had created the Good Government League (GGL) to gain advantage in municipal governance. According to one of the founders, GGL members believed they had the "best form of government, and all we needed to do was to get the right people" elected to the San Antonio City Council. Our job was to interview all current and former members of the council who had served since single-member districts were implemented in 1977.

We spent many hours that summer speaking to some very interesting people and understanding politics from a different angle. Working on this research taught me several things. It showed me how privileged citizens had manipulated the system for their own gain. It also revealed how the marginalized and disenfranchised had fought back to get proper representation. But it also forced Joaquin and me to look at fair representation for all as a struggle beyond my specific family history. Being in California had provided the space to explore and investigate my own interests, and when that experience was blended with research into my hometown politics, it changed my perspective and gave focus to my vague and unformed plans for life after Stanford.

Luis had planted a seed in the ground that Mom had been tilling since we could walk. We had been excited about helping Luis, and wanted to move beyond researching politics into actually getting involved. Joaquin and I decided to start small by running for student senate.

When we returned to Stanford for our last year, we put both our names on the election list. Our competitive nature had evolved into a mixture of pushing each other so seamlessly that an accomplishment by one of us was seen as a shared victory. We were running against each other, yet we never did any campaigning separately. It was bad enough for students figuring out whom to vote for out of all the candidates, but most of them probably couldn't even tell Joaquin and me apart. Speaking to students together may have helped matters a little, since it's always easier to tell twins apart when they're next to each other, but I have a feeling most folks saw Joaquin and me as one unit.

For a small political office, student senate had some exciting rules that fostered campaign innovation and kept the playing field level. My favorite was the strictly enforced campaign spending limit: ninety dollars. Then there were the maximum allowable days to campaign prior to the election: seven. And Stanford employed a very progressive method of voting: casting votes online.

Student senate provided one of the most important political lessons I ever learned. Joaquin and I sat down with our yellow legal pad and began brainstorming our platform. We made a very boring, predictable list with things like live shows and themed lunch menus. We didn't even know if we had the power to influence any of these ideas and never bothered looking into them since they were so unimaginative.

"What do we all need that we don't really have a structure for?" Joaquin asked. "What do we all complain about and can't find a way around, in the way Stanford is set up?"

"Dorms separated into reptilian brain and neocortex brain predispositions?" I suggested.

"Well, we'd get one vote at least."

We then looked at what our classmates struggled with rather than just asking people what they wanted.

"We need one strong thing that nobody has thought of, but they'll all recognize the need when we talk about it," I said.

It was right in front of us, but almost invisible because we'd found a solution to it already.

"I know! Better access in a more casual way for—"

"Recommendation letters!" Joaquin finished. "We all need them, and we all get freaked out and sweaty palms asking a professor for that.

"That's it," he added, satisfied.

Each dorm held a weekly residents' meeting that typically had twenty to thirty attendees, so Joaquin and I started crashing them and asking for a couple of minutes. Our routine needed a little work, starting with a bad joke before Joaquin launched into our platform.

"We'll implement what we're calling 'recommendation hours,'" he said, "a system specifically for students to meet with their professors and discuss recommendation letters, since a lot of students are too intimidated to ask."

It was illuminating, watching students getting excited about how the idea would affect their lives. Presenting something original and forward thinking that solved a specific need cut through what many regarded as boring and inconsequential politics.

We spent almost all our extra time walking the dorms, working the corridors of busy campus buildings and the lunch crowds at White Plaza, flagging down zigzagging cyclists and power walkers to hand them black-and-white campaign flyers.

The tight campaign regulations kept the candidates on a level playing field while rewarding ingenuity. For example, they didn't restrict *where* you could put campaign posters. The other candidates were posting them where everybody tacked up notices, so they had to compete with a kaleidoscope of paper announcements: "Furniture for sale!" "Movie night." "Lecture on Tuesday!"

Joaquin and I began putting up our photocopied campaign posters, but there was no way we could compete with the chaotic postings in black and white, neon green, hot pink, electric blue.

"It doesn't even matter," Joaquin said. "In about seven minutes they're going to be covered up by about ten other postings for guitar lessons and bikes for sale."

I agreed. "Nobody is going to take time to sort them out visually and then actually read these things."

I stopped pinning up posters and shifted to what I sometimes called "climbing the fence" mode. How do you get around an obstacle? We had a fence in front of us, and we could either accept that or find a way around it. We could start digging underneath. We could climb it. We could get a motor-cycle like Steve McQueen and jump it.

"Let's go get a Snapple," I said. Joaquin had the same mind-set and we knew that sitting at a picnic table drinking lemon Snapple was always a good way to clear the mind and get new ideas.

"Where do people *want* to read?" Joaquin asked about half-way through our drinks.

"Want to?"

"Yeah, like when they'll really look for something to occupy themselves," he said. "Like on an airplane — you'll read those magazines cover to cover and normally you wouldn't pick them up."

"Buses?" I suggested.

"Naw, they'd take them down in a second."

We sipped quietly for a few minutes.

"The restroom," I blurted out.

"It's gross, but people always read stuff in the restroom," Joaquin agreed.

"On the walls! When you're taking a leak! And in the stalls too!"

We visited nearly every bathroom on campus and taped the signs at eye level, well above the splash line. We even recruited some of our female friends to tape them in the girls' bathrooms.

By the end of the campaign, Joaquin and I had earned a somewhat dubious nickname: the Stall Twins. The most sur-prising aspect of the whole campaign was the result: out of forty-three candidates vying for ten seats, Joaquin and I tied for first place with 811 votes. Our political careers had officially started with a ninety-dollar campaign budget and a double victory.

With our senior year well under way, we also had to start thinking about where to go to school next. Joaquin and I had decided to go to law school—together, of course. In fact, as we applied to law schools the fall of our senior year, we made staying together our first priority. We aimed high and had solid grades, but the school application process was anything but straightforward or predictable. Brilliant friends of ours had been rejected by certain schools while other students who barely seemed awake during class breezed into the same university.

My acceptance letters came at the end of 1995. The law schools at Harvard and Stanford both accepted me, but days passed with nothing for Joaquin. His girlfriend was staying at Stanford, so that became an option for him.

I told Joaquin that I'd stay at Stanford if he got rejected by Harvard. First the White House internship divided us, and now there was this inexplicable wait. Luckily, a little less than a week later, he got the fat acceptance package from Harvard. We were going to buy winter gear for the first time in our lives. Winters in Cambridge, Massachusetts, are no joke.

In January 1996, six months shy of graduating from Stanford, Mom called to tell us that Mamo's doctors had issued a dire warning about her health. We flew home during February break and went to the hospital immediately. Mom had kept us current with Mamo's condition, but it's another thing altogether to see somebody you love seriously failing.

Mamo was fading both mentally and physically. Diabetes had finally taken its toll on her body: one foot had been amputated, and Mamo rarely got out of bed. She did get excited when we told her about college, though. For the first time, I experienced how deeply somebody can feel vicarious joy and energy from another person, especially grandkids. I have always been proud of what my brother and I accomplished in graduating high school early and getting into Stanford, but it was a different type of pride sharing that with Mamo. When we told her about tying with exactly 811 votes for student senate and about our girlfriends and our plans for the future, her eyes welled up. I felt an obligation toward her, one that wasn't restrictive like the pressure imposed as a child but a freeing and empowering one to explore all the opportunities that she hadn't been able to. I believe that, even as she was dying, my grandmother looked at her daughter and grandkids in that room and felt that her life had been a success.

Mamo's condition rapidly grew worse. The next day a doctor led Mom, my brother, and me into a small conference room down the hall from Mamo's room, and we sat down.

"Our treatments cannot sustain your mother and grandmother any longer," she said. "It's amazing that she's lasted as long as she has—a testament to her strong will. We will continue to keep her comfortable, but it's all about pain management now instead of aggressively treating anything."

After the doctor left, we stayed in the room, and a brutal silence fell as we processed what we had just heard. We stood up without looking at one another, then walked back into Mamo's room in a very different state than we had left it. Mamo was awake but looked weak. I touched her right hand and Joaquin reached for her arm, and she turned to look at us. A tear ran down her cheek. She seemed to know.

Mamo's breathing became more labored, and she fell in and out of consciousness. A priest came in to perform last rites, and by early afternoon word had spread and relatives began filling the small room.

It was crowded, and Joaquin and I conferred. We'd take the night shift together, and that would give us time alone with Mamo and for ourselves. We'd been at the hospital for many hours and told Mom we were going to take a quick break to go home and change and then come back. By the time we returned, Mamo was gone.

That night, as we sat in the house, every corner reminded Mom of a specific time with Mamo.

"Son of a bitch," Mom said. "Mamo was always talking about you two graduating college, and she was four months short of seeing you graduate."

But in some ways, Mamo's timing was nearly perfect. At eighty-two, she passed less than a year after her sister, Trinidad, and Mamo García. Her body was prepared for burial in a small plot next to Trinidad's in San Fernando Cemetery.

That night at home, I sat on my bunk bed and looked down on Mamo's daybed, still made up the way it used to be when she was with us. I thought about her life journey as an orphan from Mexico, all the stories she'd told us, all the hopes and dreams and opportunities dashed or crushed or just let loose and never chased down by her own volition. I thought about her struggles with family oppression, discrimination, opportunities cut short almost on purpose by guardians, battles with mental anxiety.

I imagined the dusty trip she made across the border as a traumatized, parentless seven-year-old, then saw her in my mind's eye moving into a stranger's house, being ripped from school and still teaching herself to read in two languages, having a baby with a barely legal man half her age, and bringing up Mom, a hell-raising civil rights fighter, and then grandkids, who, because of that long, dusty walk into the United States in 1922, were now at Stanford.

I really believe that when she smiled and cried as Joaquin and I told her about life at Stanford and our upcoming graduation, she felt she had made it—that she had realized the American dream. I have rarely felt as grateful for my life and everybody involved in it as I did that night in my bunk bed.

PART 2

Chapter Nine

Only forty-three days left," Carina said as she looked up at me across the kitchen table. I was sitting opposite my nine-year-old daughter, working on an upcoming speech for a young Democrats group. I flipped the page of my big yellow legal pad and scribbled OPEN ROAD, the germination of an idea to explore.

"Just a sec, honey," I said and added another bullet point, writing about how important it is to be open to unexpected roads in life. *Need better way to say,* I wrote next to the "road ahead" cliché. *Like Garth Brooks song "Unanswered Prayers," but not like that.* Referencing pop culture in a big speech is a delicate business. If anything, a Mars Volta song might be more appropriate for the young Democrats.

I looked across the table at my daughter.

"Sorry, what was that, Carina?"

Carina held her hands up, four fingers on her left hand, three on her right, and whispered, "Forty-three."

I gave her a puzzled look.

"Forty-three days left of school!" She raised her hands and cheered.

"Oh." In my experience, few things trigger anxiety and stress in parents as much as a child running loose for two months without a structured schedule. It's always great to see your kids get excited, but I made a mental note to talk with my wife, Erica, to see what we had planned, if anything, for our daughter. Carina obviously had expectations. Summers always had a way of sneaking up on Erica and me, especially when distracted by a lightning-fast toddler son bouncing off the walls at home.

"It's going to be fun," I said, smiling. I tapped my phone on the table to check the time: 8:20 p.m. "It's getting late. How much more homework do you have?"

Carina shuffled her papers and held up a familiar sheet with a row of dots halving the space between solid lines. "I have to practice my cursive, but I'm almost done with math."

Apparently, just talking about math is extremely exhausting, so she yawned and rubbed her eyes. I watched as she wrote the answer to 4×3.

At that moment I felt transported back to a much smaller, much messier kitchen. Mamo would be sitting there, picking apart a tortilla as she read one of her beloved Agatha Christie mysteries. Her thumb held one side open as the pages fanned out, curled at the edges, the cover torn, and apparently one of her cats had chewed a corner of the binding down to a rounded pulp.

Everything about Mamo had that look. She never had much,

but what she had, whether it was a favorite robe or a favorite book or a favorite mixing bowl, was well worn with love.

Carina put a strip of a torn tortilla in her mouth and did that telltale eye rub. Then she answered the last math question on the page and tapped her pencil with a flourish. How Mamo would have loved to have been doing homework at my daughter's age.

"Is school that bad?" I asked.

"It's okay, but summer is way better."

Another eye rub.

"Summer is pretty cool," I had to admit. "But I actually liked school."

"Did you know you wanted to go to Harvard and be a lawyer and then do the White House thing when you were my age?"

"At age nine? Third grade?" I paused. "Yeah, I had my life pretty planned out by then."

"Really?"

I nodded. "I knew *exactly* what I wanted to be."

An image of Joaquin and me sitting in our bedroom flashed in my mind. "I was going to be a professional wrestler. My master plan was to be like Randall Cunningham except actually win the Super Bowl."

"Who's that?"

"He used to play for Daddy's favorite football team way before you were born."

"Football is so boring."

"My nine-year-old self disagrees with you," I replied. "Anyway, I learned to be open to things in life, even when they don't necessarily work out how you planned. Instead, I got to become a lawyer and then marry your mom and get elected mayor of San Antonio and then have you and then work for President Obama in Washington."

Carina looked at me, suspicious that this was turning into some sort of lesson.

"You know," I said, "I think Mom's ambition was to be a football player too."

"No! Mom said she always wanted to be a teacher."

I shrugged. "Maybe I did get that wrong. Well, she could've been a good quarterback too."

I tapped her cursive sheet. "But I did like school. I liked how it gave me a sense of control over my future. I liked how it seemed to open up so many possibilities. And, unlike you, I didn't really like math. Let's get this done and get to bed."

"You're not even big enough to play football, Daddy. Good thing you did something else!" she exclaimed.

"It's a good thing I did well in school."

Looking back, my family's story almost feels like a lab experiment in the difference an education makes. My grandmother never forgave the theft of her education, and her daughter watched as that lack of education boxed her mother into a life of menial jobs. The daughter in turn struggled to raise us and stay above the poverty line, but she still found a way to complete her master's degree. Joaquin and I skipped a grade to graduate early while almost a third of our high school classmates dropped out. Then we traveled as a pair to one of the top law schools in the country, even though few in our social orbit had trod that path before. Being open and at the same time pushing oneself to get an education can be as beneficial as the education itself.

But part of that education is knowing how to fit the pursuit of knowledge into a balanced life. Mamo's death made us reconsider the immediate future. We'd been away for four taxing years and always considered San Antonio home. We were nervous about the notoriously demanding three years that awaited us in law school and felt emotionally drained. After Joaquin and I were accepted into Harvard, we decided to take a year off and be at home with Mom.

At home again, in my bunk bed again, there was a natural instinct to sort out who I was now. I had left home as an eager student in a modest Mexican American neighborhood, matured at Stanford, where I was exposed to different cultures from around the world, had a girlfriend, Nisha, who was now across the country, and was preparing for a three-year tour in one of the most rigorous law schools in the world.

I owed eighteen thousand dollars in student loans, so I thought I might chip away at the debt while I tried to figure things out and get used to life without Mamo. Mom and Dad had both been teachers, and while the low pay and school politics could be taxing, they loved the interaction with their students. I ran the idea of taking a substitute teaching job by Mom.

"I liked teaching. You feel like you're contributing to a child's future success," she said. "It's a lot harder work than you might think, though, Julián. But it's incredibly rewarding."

I knew from my own experience that a teacher could make a profound difference in the life of a student. One day in the first grade, my teacher took me aside after class and opened the workbook to a page far ahead of what she had assigned.

"Julián, can you do up to page fifty-seven in your workbook? You're doing very well, and I think you can handle it."

That night, I sacrificed the *Dukes of Hazzard* and other TV shows to complete the extra work.

I had stuck my pencil in the workbook when I finished, and when the teacher came in, I walked up to her desk and opened the book to that page. "I finished up to page fifty-seven!" I told her, all smiles.

"I knew you would," she answered. "Let's go up to page seventy-five tonight."

Wait a sec. Did I just get played? It seemed ridiculous, but I actually loved doing the work. It wasn't the extra effort that mattered, either; it was how the assignments gave me confidence that I was a good student. I began to take pride in doing the assignments well, and soon I knew that I could excel in school. That first-grade teacher was the kind of teacher I wanted to be.

I applied for and was offered a job as a substitute teacher with the San Antonio Independent School District. The pay was bad—about fifty-five dollars a day, slightly above the amount Mamo would have earned for cleaning houses if she had been working then. I didn't know a thing about teaching but decided I could wing it, having been a student for most of my life. I'd watched more than a few teachers through the years and suffered under some poor ones, and at the very least I figured I could do the job better than they had.

I taught a few classes as a substitute, and a few weeks into the school year, right as I turned twenty-two, I was offered and eagerly accepted a semester-long teaching spot at Jefferson, my old school. Before I got started, I met with a district executive, a veteran teacher who had moved into administration. She looked me over, noting my age and inexperience, and gave me one piece of advice: "Don't try to be friends with the students — be their teacher."

What? No way, I was going to be a beacon shining bright for these kids. I had some serious *Stand and Deliver, Dead Poets Society* drive going right then.

It's a warped feeling as a teacher to walk the same hallways of a school you couldn't wait to get out of as a student. I was just four years older than the seniors, yet felt incredibly old for the first time in my life. Was I an adult? I didn't feel like a kid, but it was as if I was wearing a teacher costume. I may have been fooling the authorities, but not the kids with their BS sensors.

I took over two speech classes and a world geography class as a "permanent sub," one of the most neutered titles available as a teacher. A permanent sub doesn't have the advantage of coming in for one day, offering a welcome break for the class, and then getting out of Dodge before the students can take advantage of your inexperience. A permanent sub has all the responsibilities of a permanent teacher without any of the authority.

Nearly all of my students were Mexican American, and most of them came from the same type of neighborhood I grew up in. Even on the best days, the classes were far too large to offer many opportunities for one-on-one connection. One class had thirty-seven students, another thirty-eight, and the last one was thirty-nine. I instinctively divided the class into three sections: loners who needed to be drawn out; attention seekers who covered insecurities by acting tough or being the class clown; and eager students focusing—sometimes even excessively—on grades.

But, especially as a newbie, I was learning just as much from my students. A few weeks in, I turned to write on the blackboard and a paper ball hit me on the back of the head.

I have to admit, it was a good shot. I paused, feeling that I was suddenly given a pop quiz I had not studied for. I stared at my chalk, pressing it against the blackboard knowing I had to answer somehow by the time I turned around. For a split second, I wondered whether I could pretend like nothing happened, play it off and save my dignity.

Then the class burst into laughter, knowing that my immediate reaction already allowed a window of safety.

I turned around.

"All right, who threw that?"

Was I that far removed that I thought a teenager would rat a classmate out? They had all been laughing at me a second ago.

What do you do when you're staring at a class, humiliated by some scrunched-up piece of paper? I failed badly. Not knowing how to handle that wasn't just a mistake, it affected how the class saw me, including those students who were taking class seriously. It felt like I'd lost considerable authority in the eyes of all my students.

But I was learning. The district administrator's advice had been right, and I became a drill sergeant. Keep quiet, pay attention, or get out. Once I had the students' respect, I gradually eased up and related to them as someone who had been in those seats just a few years earlier, someone who wanted to see them achieve their dreams just as I was achieving mine.

That was my first lesson as a teacher: how to create the proper environment. Sometimes, toward the end of class, I asked my students where they hoped to find themselves in five years. Most of the students didn't have the support I had with Mom, and even the most motivated ones picked lower-hanging careers they wanted to pursue, aiming a notch just below a professional job—lab technician, paralegal, physical therapist. What about a doctor? Lawyer? Engineer? Those careers were barely mentioned.

I thought about my classmates at Stanford and imagined what their answers would have been. Most people set their horizons based on examples in their surrounding environment. The young people in my community were not being exposed to the complete span of education or professions, and they understandably set their expectations accordingly. Besides the actual educational component of school, there is a need to show all students how limitless their potential is if they focus. At their age, Joaquin and I saw ourselves going to college and achieving big things, and even if it was just a fantasy at the time, we acted as if it could be a reality and worked toward it.

I don't get down very often, but I did begin to feel sad about some of my students. There were so many eager and bright kids, but they'd turn in written work that was not only weak but verging on illiterate. Test scores were mediocre at best. This wasn't the students' fault, so I started encouraging them not to limit their education to what was taught in the classroom.

The internet was making it possible to seek out answers independently, and I used myself as an example of a kid in their exact circumstances who got into one of the best schools in the country, as well as the Jefferson kid in a class ahead of me who got into Harvard. We were proof that it could be done.

I had to find ways to slip this message in without sounding preachy or full of myself. I began involving some students more actively, calling on them and making them realize they were smart enough to become a doctor or engineer or lawyer. I started to feel a growing openness and excitement to learn. The difference? The students could see it all leading to something now. School was a necessary ingredient in achieving a dream.

Teaching is one of the most creative and exhausting jobs I have ever had. Clever political adversaries, irate constituents, and elbow-throwing litigators were never as tough to handle as those students were on a daily basis. Every day after work I would drive home feeling like I needed a five-hour nap just to recover from the school day. Permanent subbing gave me a whole new level of respect for teachers as professionals. It taught me that not just anyone can teach. It's a craft that takes skill, patience, and the right personality in order to effectively convey knowledge and manage a classroom.

It hurts to admit, but I didn't have those abilities at the time. I was not the teacher my students deserved. If you've been a good employee or a good boss or a good student, sometimes people will come up to you and tell you that. "Man, you were a good mayor," I sometimes hear from folks in San Antonio. In the more than twenty years since I taught those classes, not one student has ever come up to me and said, "Hey, you were great," or "I enjoyed your class." Hasn't happened. I simply wasn't prepared to succeed at the time. I'd like to think that if I'd stayed in the profession I would have learned how to be successful. But either way, I learned from that experience the importance of always being prepared for what you tackle, no matter how simple or straightforward it might seem.

By spring the school district found a permanent teacher to take over my classes. The timing was perfect, since I had to start thinking about law school and shifting back to a student mindset.

Joaquin, meanwhile, had been working in San Antonio's municipal Office of Special Projects, and the director, Frances Gonzalez, offered me a position to fill until I left for Harvard. The office oversaw intergovernmental affairs, youth initiatives, and neighborhood revitalization—a trifecta that once again aligned with what Mom had fought for at our age. The city had previously organized a project called the Parade of Homes, working with affordable housing developers to create infill neighborhoods in the urban core of the city, an area long neglected by builders.

Now it was preparing its second Parade of Homes on the city's East Side, which offered an opportunity for first-time homebuyers of modest means to live in a new house in the neighborhood they'd grown up in. The development represented the kind of positive future that was possible if the city and private sector worked together.

As administrative assistants, Joaquin and I attended meetings and events, getting into the guts of government and working from the inside. We helped plan the opening for the Parade of Homes, speaking with families who had benefited from the first round. This was the closest I'd ever been to real public-sector work, and I became fascinated by how the city government worked and by its capacity to help people.

Seeing the joy of these families as they talked about their new neighborhood really affected me, and it connected a distant policy proposal with real life. I not only saw but *felt* the tangible benefit of public service, especially of local government, because it dealt in tangible outcomes — creating housing opportunity, improving streets, making neighborhoods safe. I may not have been a great teacher right away, but I was good at this job and it was something that could also improve the lives of folks like my old students at Jefferson and their families. Experience is a vital aspect of education, and just as I had tried to expand opportunities for my students, I entered Harvard Law School with a very different sense of what I wanted to do when I left.

Growing up in San Antonio and going to college in California did nothing to prepare me for Cambridge winters. We had never visited Stanford or Harvard before applying to the schools, so our sense of the environment was limited to magazine articles and pictures in the application brochures and on the internet. I didn't buy my first real winter coat until I was twenty-three.

But my worry about a frigid winter paled in comparison to my anxiety over Harvard Law School. Joaquin and I were assigned rooms down the hall from each other in Shaw Hall, a campus dorm, and that helped take some of the edge off. But there was still a lot of edge left. The school had a reputation as an intellectual boot camp designed to break and weed out the unworthy. It was also known as one of the most competitive schools in the world. I was told that students routinely tore pages out of important books in the law school library so that others couldn't complete their assignments. If the teachers didn't get you, then the students would, or so I was led to believe.

I'd watched the movie *The Paper Chase,* about the infamous pressures Harvard students deal with (one of the characters commits suicide), and read the critical book *Broken Contract: A Memoir of Harvard Law,* which explores how a high percentage of students enter with the plan to go into public interest law but end up working in the much more lucrative and ruthless realm of corporate law. In the movie, the main character is asked, in front of the class and on the first day, to answer a difficult question. He doesn't know the answer, and later vomits into a trash can from the stress. Even when I watched the movie, I rolled my eyes at the dramatic license, but it didn't exactly ease my nerves about the place.

On the first day, one of my professors, Martha Minow, who would go on to be the dean of the law school, welcomed us into the large, theater-style classroom and explained, in one brief, terror-filled greeting, how the Socratic teaching method would work. After introducing herself, she pointed to a brown-haired guy in a green polo shirt. "In five minutes I'm going to call on you," she told him.

I have never been happier not to be somebody in my entire

life. I could feel a sense of relief spring up in the classroom—well, except for the guy she'd called on. He shuffled his reading notes uncomfortably as the rest of us thanked our lucky stars.

By the time I finished law school, I had fully experienced the anxiety people often project about moving up to the next level in life. That fear doesn't have to end in hitting your stomach's eject button, but it can derail your life if you don't push through it. I recall the fear I felt back in sixth grade when the administrator at Rhodes questioned how many of us would make it through middle school. I didn't stress out heavily, but I did start worrying about how hard it was going to be. When I was in high school and applying to college, I kept hearing from friends that you needed to study three hours for every hour you were in class. I did the math. If I was in class for six hours a day, that meant eighteen hours of studying. That's twenty-four hours.

All these fears mounted into one essential question: Was I good enough? I've had that stressful, throwing-up feeling—that trash can moment—in life, and now I recognize it as the folly of freaking out based on untrue myths about the difficulty of the next level in life.

Harvard Law School wasn't hell, but it was very taxing and not always fun. Still, it was manageable. By our second and third years, Joaquin and I had set our pace and were able to find time and energy to pursue other interests.

Not freaking out about law school allowed me the chance to reflect on my tenure as an earnest but greenhorn teacher. I might be hefting a heavy law book off a library shelf when suddenly I'd think back to Jefferson and a student who had asked a question with a curiosity and eagerness that could either be slowly smothered or encouraged so that she would level up. I'd sit in the library, pausing now and then as I grew frustrated for that student and many others. They needed to know that they could be here if they put in the work and if they understood the pathway, the structure, that would get them here.

If you live in an environment brimming with examples of achievement, then it's understandable why you'd think that success has to do only with effort and attitude. If you have a touchstone, an adviser available to answer and encourage and connect you with other helpers, then you still have to do the work, but there is a support system in place that makes success more likely.

I've heard so often that people attribute success just to working incredibly hard to realize their goals, but some people have to work just as hard while also blazing a new path, and that extra work not only takes a lot of energy but can foster a fear of the next phase. If you can see your uncle or neighbor at the next level of achievement, it is vastly different from peering up into an unknown, seemingly hostile, and more demanding stage of life. I'd known many smart young people with talent and ambition in my hometown, but they lacked access to opportunities or somebody from that higher level offering a hand to pull them up.

"We need to get more people from neighborhoods like ours here," I said to Joaquin one day as we watched TV in his room.

"What, start a scholarship?"

"Yeah, right after we pay off our own mountain of school debt," I said. "No, something that exposes them to the possibilities. I saw so many kids in my class at Jefferson that could cut it here. But I could tell that if I told them that they'd laugh.

"I wonder, what's the percentage of students here that had lawyers or other professionals in their family?"

Joaquin thought about our pool of friends. "Pretty high, for sure. The good thing is that most of them seem willing to help people who don't have the same advantages."

Far from vindictive jerks who ripped out pages in library law books, my classmates were almost all thoughtful and engaged. And nice. "Why not ask them to help now?"

Joaquin looked at me questioningly.

"Now we have so many ways to connect—with email and the internet. Distance doesn't matter as much; these kids want to go to law school, and we can pair them with some of the best law students in the country. Why wait until you have a law degree? Let's make it easy right now. I don't think it would take much to encourage some of the kids from San Antonio, especially when another successful older student is supporting them."

Three days later, Joaquin sat down next to me in the dining hall. "Electronic Partnership of Aspiring Law Students—E-PALS. That's it," he said.

"Nice! That is a simple name that explains it all."

E-PALS became an informal, email-based pen pal project between students at Harvard Law School and those in the law studies magnet program at Fox Tech High School in the San Antonio Independent School District. Email was a standard form of communication, especially among younger people, so it required very little beyond pairing people up. The students at Harvard were not that much older than the students at Fox Tech, and the law students quickly drew inspiration from their new pen pals in a vastly dissimilar environment. Scholastically, though, it was like two aliens talking to each other from distant planets.

"Holy shit," one of my classmates said one day. "My pen pal has never even met a lawyer in real life."

Just as the kids in San Antonio were being exposed to a new world, so were many of the students in Cambridge, and I could see the impact of this personal connection. The Harvard students may have been some of the brightest in law school, but they also were deeply sympathetic to kids who lacked the opportunities that many of them had assumed most people had.

More and more classmates became involved with E-PALS. Several dozen people participated on each end, and it was easy to set up. And once the simple idea was hatched, people *wanted* to participate.

We need to find more opportunities for small projects like this that cultivate ambition. All of us can help others grow in so many ways in life. We can all start doing small things to reach down and pull somebody up, just as so many people did along the way for Joaquin and me.

Perhaps my DNA makes me more susceptible to the political bug, but shortly after starting law school, I started thinking about what to do next. I knew I was going back to San Antonio — that was home — but I knew I wouldn't be happy just practicing law. I also felt an obligation to help others in my neighborhood be able to reach their own dreams.

As much progress as the West Side of San Antonio had made since my mother and her contemporaries began their fight to improve the quality of life there, the neighborhoods I grew up in still suffered from higher dropout rates, higher unemployment, worse infrastructure, and less investment than the neighborhoods my grandmother had traveled by bus to work in. For me, law wasn't just about winning a case—it was about actively doing something about an injustice.

A very smart professor once told my class at Harvard that "law is about distinguishing between fact patterns and situations. There is a body of law that governs what people can and cannot do in our society, but the ultimate determination comes down to the factual circumstances of each case as they compare to the established law." This characterization might work in a court of law, but there was also a much larger set of social circumstances at play, and these tended to rig the system and create injustice. Politics and policy are often needed to right those wrongs on a larger scale.

Working with my brother for the Office of Special Projects in San Antonio the summer before law school, I saw how government can transform a community. Government has the ability to keep the city streets clean and safe, provide high-quality education and job training, make social services productive and empowering, and build affordable housing like the units I'd seen go up on the East Side.

The distance that I'd recently traveled in life provided perspective on the obstacles that remained in my hometown. I appreciated even more how Mom and Dad had worked so hard to increase political participation among the people who were most often left behind. The local community, the cities, and the state and federal government would become much more responsive to vulnerable communities if participation increased on all levels.

A sizable chip formed on my shoulder while studying at Harvard. Now that I was able to compare my hometown to another dynamic, entrepreneurial community, this time on the East Coast, I grew more convinced that San Antonio could be much more. The community deserved more, and I believed I had a vision for the city's future and a talent for public service that could benefit my old neighborhoods and the entire city tremendously. The idea of a run for office of some kind began to take shape.

But I had reservations. Politics had a bad reputation. It could be personal and ugly. It could be divisive. And it could be expensive too. How in the world would I get the money to run a campaign? Mom had been an outsider in politics, I thought, and although she ultimately helped make progress in the community, she didn't come anywhere close to winning an election. Then again, that was 1971, almost thirty years earlier. Some things had changed. As Luis had told Joaquin and me at Stanford, today young Latinos running for office had so much more opportunity to garner the support of a broad base of people of different backgrounds.

Should I go into politics or shouldn't I? Joaquin and I spent many months discussing this during law school.

"Should we work on the outside or the inside?" I asked, without knowing the answer. "Which is more effective at this point?"

Politics can be similar to a funhouse mirror—there's always a danger of believing that the warped reflection is reality. I wondered whether winning in politics would require me to turn into someone I wasn't. Would I have to be louder or nastier or act like a know-it-all even when I didn't have all the answers? I'm naturally introverted, and politics rarely rewards those who stay withdrawn while running a campaign, so what would it do to me if I felt forced to act a certain way to win? Worse still, would I have to bend my principles to succeed?

We have all seen it happen. The prospect of winning an election proves so tempting that otherwise genuine people make compromises to come out on top. There are numerous examples of minority politicians announcing that they would "take it to the man," only to slide right into a corporation's pocket. Often, the loudest and most blustery are the quickest to fold. The desire to stay in office or the need to raise funds can overpower the drive to push for reforms that might better the lives of the people the officials were elected to represent.

Ultimately, I was able to overcome these reservations because I felt anchored by my roots, especially the legacy of my mother's activism, and I was confident enough in myself to believe that I could be different, that I could resist those temptations altogether.

It also helped that there was already an example of somebody near my age who had leveled up. In 1997, a few months before I had left for law school, Ed Garza, a twenty-seven-year-old urban planner and Texas A&M University graduate, had been elected to city council in the district where I grew up.

Because of term limits, his tenure would end in 2001, about a year after I graduated from law school. I made a commitment to myself to pursue the seat he would vacate. Now I just had to figure out how to run for office.

The one thing I never expected is that my decision to run for city council would provide me with the most effective pickup line of my life. After our second year at Harvard, Joaquin and I decided to work as summer associates at the law firm of Akin Gump, spending half the summer in its San Antonio office and the other half in Austin. Nisha and I had drifted apart with the help of a few thousand miles, but I had always been fine alone, so I was in no hurry to start dating again.

I really missed Texas, and I wasn't aware of how homesick I was until I came home during that summer break. The second year of law school lacks the excitement of the first year and the anticipation of graduation in the third year. I was pretty comfortable with law school by this time and couldn't wait to get back home.

The night Joaquin and I flew in, we connected with our old friend Celso and went to the Fox & Hound, a new restaurant and bar on the city's northwest side. It was late and I was burned out from the flight, but while waiting for a table in a line that was taking way too long to move, I began noticing the long black hair of the girl in front of me. The head of hair belonged to a five-foot-seven Filipino girl with a slender build who was wearing a black tube top and khaki pants. I was in trouble.

I did nothing. I'll tell you right now, and this is from real-world experience: it's a lot easier to run for mayor or speak to a president than it is to say *anything* to a girl you just fell for at a restaurant. The next morning I had a knot in my stomach and felt nauseated. I knew I'd made a mistake in letting her get away, but I had no idea how to reach her. Luckily, Celso came to the rescue. Turns out he had dated one of her friends. I gushed to him about the Filipino girl, and a few days later he called me with a dossier of intel, which he shared with me as I sat on my old bed at Mom's.

"Back in the old bunk beds, huh?"

"For now," I said. "It's actually kind of a drastically up-and-down feeling. Sometimes it's comforting and other times this voice in my head is almost shaming me, but for now it's good."

Of course, the house didn't feel the same at all since Mamo's death. It felt empty, lacking the presence of the biggest personality in our family.

We sat quietly for a few seconds. I was thinking of how Celso used to come over, and we'd play Super Mario Brothers for hours in the living room under Mamo's watchful eye. Right then, even as everything in my life was in flux, I felt very lucky to have grown up the way I did.

"So, her name is Erica," Celso said, cutting through the silence. "She grew up on the South Side of San Antonio and just finished her sophomore year at the University of Texas at San Antonio. My friend thinks you guys would like each other, be a good fit. Says she's smart and similar to you in a lot of ways. Personally, I'd think that's a deal breaker, but maybe there's still time for her to change."

"Yeah, yeah. What else?"

"I got her number."

A flash of adrenaline hit me.

"Okay, okay, okay," I said to myself.

"Are you talking to yourself?" Celso said.

I hung up with him, grabbed a notepad, and began organizing my thoughts on paper, roughing out bullet points for the conversation.

I jotted down a few notes so as not to forget. It wasn't *exactly* an outline, but—well, yes, it was basically an outline. I can't really defend that. I was really stressed, and providing structure always helped calm me down. Some people write love letters to melt someone's heart; this time I just had to sketch out a rough script.

"Am I really this pathetic?" I thought to myself. "Jotting down notes for a phone call to ask someone out?"

Thankfully, it worked. Erica agreed to meet me for dinner. We had our first date at Mi Tierra, a well-known restaurant in the historic Market Square district downtown. Erica arrived early, so when I got there I first saw her sitting on a bench inside the restaurant's lobby. Wearing jeans and a pink top with her long black hair pulled back, she looked perfect to me. I felt a flush of excitement as I walked up to her.

"Hi, I'm Julián. Are you Erica?" I introduced myself.

"Hi! Yes, I am. Thanks for keeping me waiting," she shot back.

"Oh, sorry! Have you been here long?"

"I'm kidding."

We were soon shown to a table, where we ordered our

drinks and kept up some small talk. So far, so good. Then things went downhill fast. The waiter came back to our table and turned to Erica.

"What can I get you, ma'am?"

"Oh, I'm not going to eat. I'll just have this drink."

What? Why wouldn't she order anything? My mind started racing. Naturally, I assumed that she took one look at me and quickly submarined the dinner to end the date ASAP.

I ordered the largest plate of nachos in the state of Texas and planned to eat slowly to build a case for myself. She ended up sharing the plate, just like Lady and the Tramp, except the Mexicana version, over nachos instead of spaghetti.

Celso's friend was right—we were a good match. Not because we both liked nachos but because, as Erica later told me, my passionate speech about trying to get elected to a city council seat that paid twenty dollars a month aligned with many of her feelings about why she wanted to teach elementary school.

I hadn't planned on talking about any of my political ambitions. I was still self-conscious about them and had instead intended to dazzle her with stories about Harvard, giving her a sense that I had a bright future. But the conversation naturally led to discussing our aspirations, and I felt safe with her, so I opened up.

"After I pass the bar, I'll start practicing law and try and get on the city council and then become mayor."

She was silent. It was May 26, 1999, and I was twenty-four years old. The city council election was still two years away, but I had already begun roughing out a campaign.

Her almond eyes were not Filipino, as I had thought, but

Latino. Either way, they looked intimidating as I tried to read them. Was I full of BS? Was I beyond boring? Or was I ambitious to make change and help others?

"Do you really believe you can do that?" she asked.

"Yeah, I do."

It was important to have somebody besides family believing in my dreams. Erica was just as motivated about her career as my brother and I were about ours, and she fit into our relationship with ease.

I knew several bitter lawyers who were hugely successful and miserable at their jobs without even knowing why. So I made a pledge to myself to find a balance between my professional life and political ambitions before I found myself in too deep. I would pass the bar, make a very good living as a lawyer, buy a house, and pay off my eighty thousand dollars in student debt. Then I'd adjust my life accordingly as I held a city council seat and ran for mayor. I had learned from some of the best teachers in the country how to be a great lawyer, and they had prepared me well enough to leave ample creativity, energy, and passion for learning how to become an effective political agent of change.

Already, my professional and political lives were crossing in ways that signaled a positive future. José Villarreal, a partner in Akin Gump's San Antonio corporate practice group, had recruited Joaquin and me to join the firm. Villarreal began as a civil rights lawyer, became active in the Clinton-Gore campaign, briefly worked as deputy director of White House personnel in the Clinton administration, and then served as treasurer of the Gore campaign in 2000. He even knew Mom from her civil rights days. Villarreal was a key supporter at the firm and in politics as I sought to balance both my political and professional ambitions.

I bought a fixer-upper house with Akin Gump's signing bonus. Joaquin moved in, only this time we didn't have to sleep in bunk beds.

My time in college and law school was done, but my education was far from over. Running for office, any office, involves a steep learning curve. It requires the ability to read people, an understanding of issues important to voters, and the ability to communicate well. Politics also brings to life the blunt and brutal reality of the infamous saying about "almost": It only counts in horseshoes and hand grenades. And that little bit of truth can make for some serious stress.

I began campaigning on Election Day 2000, seven months ahead of the city council election. Ed Garza had an heir apparent, and there was lots of interest in the seat. The presidential campaign would become infamous when a razor-thin vote margin in Florida between George W. Bush and Vice President Al Gore required recounts and was ultimately decided by the Supreme Court.

My theory is that when running for office, a candidate needs to tell folks in simple terms what he or she stands for. I had shaved my initial list down and had two easy-to-understand phrases: smart growth and a knowledge economy.

I had my stump speech set on auto repeat and I would engage at almost any interaction. "Hi, I'm Julián Castro. I'm running for city council because I believe we should pursue a smart growth, knowledge economy agenda to create opportunity in twenty-first-century industries and give neighborhood residents a say in shaping the character of their neighborhoods."

Joaquin spent his spare time handing out flyers, organizing block walks, and knocking on doors. It felt a lot like the campaign we had run at Stanford together, except it was just me on the ballot and we had a lot more area to cover than just bathroom stalls.

The city council race taught Joaquin and me the value of getting in front of people, making a human connection. If you can look people in the eye and learn to genuinely listen and communicate, then they will engage. And, as I found out, people want to know how you can improve life not just for them but for their neighbors as well. Overwhelmingly, they wanted to be part of a prosperous community.

Experiencing politics firsthand also taught me how gratifying it can be. I spoke to neighborhood associations, parent-teacher associations, union gatherings, small businesses, and on front porches and doorsteps.

One of the biggest lessons I learned was that allowing people to get emotional issues off their chest often set up a productive conversation. But to do that, you had to listen and realize when you were wrong. I witnessed so many examples of angry, hardened cynics coming into a conversation hot and then giving you a moment to make your case, and if you were genuine, even if they didn't agree, they engaged in a conversation instead of name calling or shouting and shutting the mental door. I also heard about people's dreams. Lots of dreams and aspirations—sometimes undisguised and sometimes right there between the lines of conversation.

I'd point in the direction of one of my old houses.

"I grew up right over there and went to Jefferson," I'd say. "My mom always encouraged my brother and me to pursue our dreams. That's why we aimed high and got into college and law school, and why I'm running for city council right now. I want more people from my neighborhood to do the same in their own way."

I launched my campaign in a place as close to a concrete metaphor as possible. Los Colorines was an old gas station renovated into a restaurant and located in a ramshackle neighborhood from the 1920s. The area was ignored until the 1990s, when neighborhood residents and business owners began mining all the cool aspects of it and renovating one structure after another until it became known as the Deco District. And how cool was this: the city declared it a revitalization project and pitched in money and resources. This was what I liked to see: people rebuilding their neighborhoods without forgetting their past, and creating new opportunity.

The campaign quickly became a full-time job, the only problem being that I already had a full-time job as a baby lawyer in Akin Gump's litigation practice. It took less than two weeks for me to realize that I was not better off carrying the workload of both jobs. I'd be knocking on doors, attending meetings, and doing research work at home, plus spending all day writing about and discussing legal cases. I was just waiting for those purple cystic zits to erupt all over my face again.

I had no choice but to own up to being overwhelmed. Luckily, my mentor at Akin Gump was heavily into politics and thoroughly understood. I had made a promise to the firm that I needed to amend, so in spring 2001 I proposed that if I won election in May I would take on a three-quarters workload for a three-quarters paycheck. Before I sound too heroic, I'll confess that the starting salary for a first-year associate was one hundred and ten thousand dollars.

"Cast your vote for the future." I'd come across the slogan years earlier when I was researching Henry Cisneros's groundbreaking 1981 mayoral victory. One of the local newspapers—back in the days of two-newspaper towns—used the expression as the headline for its endorsement of Henry. I thought it matched my youth and my focus on the city's future and adopted the slogan for my campaign.

Some of Mom's old friends from her Chicano movement days became regular volunteers at the improvised campaign headquarters—my fixer-upper. They made phone calls and stamped envelopes. The garage was full of campaign signs and boxes of pamphlets and mailers. A brigade of college students from St. Mary's University, which sat in the district, fanned out to knock on doors during weekends that spring. My friends from Harvard flew into town to help. Those classmates, many of them involved in E-PALS, showed me how naturally energizing a political campaign can be if it's something you truly believe in. They weren't even from Texas and wouldn't directly benefit, yet back in Cambridge they hosted my first fundraiser and collected almost two thousand dollars.

And then there was Mom, Rosie Castro from the barrio, veteran of so many uphill campaigns, making calls from her home and mine, activating her old network. We didn't agree on every issue, but she was very excited.

"I never imagined that we would be there doing this together," she once said. It was one of those emotionally teary moments, but really, what did she expect? She had found a way around the age-old question of nature versus nurture rather than taking her chances.

The district I sought to represent stretched from the city's working-class West Side to newer areas in its Northwest corridor. I addressed basic infrastructure issues like potholes and traffic flow but signaled an eagerness to work on these issues as part of a larger strategy to increase the city's economic growth and improve residents' quality of life.

It helped that the election was nonpartisan, so I didn't have to take a preconceived "side" on any issue and could formulate my own ideas based on talking to people. When I showed up at someone's doorstep, that voter could consider my candidacy without the bias that party affiliation brings. Voters started the conversation curious and talked much more freely. Local government touches people's lives in a tangible way—streets, sidewalks, public safety, job creation—so it was easy to find something people cared about.

The filing deadline was in March, and six other candidates had filed for the seat, but none could keep up with our army of volunteers. We knocked on more doors, called more voters, and delivered a more powerful message than my opponents did. To each of the candidates' credit, the tone of the campaign was civil. I didn't go negative, and the only real pushback against my candidacy centered on my youth, the one thing I couldn't do anything about. I had a good laugh when one of my opponents copied the basic design of my yard sign except that above his picture was the word "Experience." Whether I was in a classroom at my old high school or in the middle of my first campaign, I couldn't avoid the consequences of looking younger than some people thought I should.

Election day was May 5, Cinco de Mayo, a traditional day of celebration among Mexican Americans in observance of Mexico's victory over France. Mom, Joaquin, Erica, Celso, my high school and law school friends, and dozens of young and old volunteers hung out with me to await the results. I won with almost 62 percent of the vote.

As I spoke to supporters that night, I thought about how, thirty years earlier, Mom had also been awaiting election results, but they didn't turn out to be cause for celebration. She and her activist, Baby Boomer contemporaries had run in 1971 to close the gap in opportunity and quality of life that plagued San Antonio's East, South, and West Sides, which were mostly Latino and black. On the night she lost the election, she told a local reporter, "We'll be back." Afterward, she went back to volunteering and working to help change the democratic process for the better, to make it more inclusive, more reflective of the community as a whole. By the time I ran in 2001, our country and our city had made a lot of progress. I saw my victory that night as one more example of that progress, and I knew that Mom's efforts and the efforts of so many others like her were one of the reasons her son was celebrating a victory.

We also celebrated Mom's upcoming birthday that evening, and the crowd sang "Happy Birthday" as she blew out a single candle on her cake. She'd made a lot of wishes in her fifty-four years, and I hoped she'd realized that one of them had come true: she had made a difference.

It was time for me to learn how to become an elected official. I had completed my formal education, but I was well aware that now I had opened myself up to an entirely new way of learning—out in the political wild, rather than in a sheltered classroom.

Chapter Ten

I think I'm done with politics," I said into the microphone held out in front of my face, emphasizing that I'd just lost the election.

"You won't regroup and think about running again?"

I looked up and channeled into the microphone the emotions I felt blowing through me.

"No."

That night in June 2005 is a fog, and I can't even remember who the reporter said she worked for. But she was good, and kept getting sound bites.

"As the projected frontrunner of the mayoral election, this must come as something of a surprise," she said.

I thought about her question—a surprise? Oh, I still had that inward stare where I wasn't blinking too much.

"Can you walk us through how the night developed for you and your team?"

Could I? As that aforementioned frontrunner, election night

had unfolded in slow agony, as if my political skin were slowly being flayed in public until the final results were announced: my opponent, retired judge Phil Hardberger, had won 51.5 percent of the vote.

In my experience, losing in politics is unlike losing at anything else. A whole city had a choice between me and the other guy, and they'd chosen the other guy. There was the sense of failure, which hurt, and then a worse feeling—that you let down so many people who supported you. The thousands of hopeful supporters posting signs with your name front and center; all the people you've shaken hands with, who have wished you well, who have dug into their own pockets to donate because they believe in you...you feel horrible for letting them down. And then you discover that along with that sting of disappointment comes levels of embarrassment far deeper than you ever imagined.

In your electoral district, your face, for a time, personifies losing. The chatty guy you buy your breakfast from every morning nods and shrugs a lot the morning following the defeat, speaking in halting sentences because he doesn't know what to say when he's been wishing you victory for the past three months.

"Next time, huh?"

"There won't be a next time," I say, meaning it. Did I sound strong, as if I had always been prepared for this defeat? I don't think so, but I tried. Then my emotions swiveled unpredictably into a defiant sense of rejecting the pain. I'm a lawyer, I tell myself in the car. I can just practice law.

But you only lost by 1.5 percent, a voice says, small and

distant in my head. *A lot of people believed in you and supported you. That is something amazing to experience, whether you won or lost.*

I have a friend who knows a professional baseball player, and one time this ball player explained how barely losing a game was so much more painful than an embarrassing blowout. The close ones kept him up at night. "All I can do is think about the little things I might have done differently," he said. "I can't stop replaying all the little plays that would have made the smallest difference and allowed us to win."

The ball player knew what he was talking about. That night after the election was a sleepless exercise in replaying my entire campaign. Erica tried to stay up and keep me company, but I was miserable and uncommunicative, and she fell asleep on the sofa as I stared off into the bottomless depths of defeat.

The next morning, as I drove to my office, I thought about all the people who had supported me during the campaign and wished me well as it progressed. Maybe it wasn't all negative.

Then I drove past a Castro for Mayor sign stuck in the grass.

Screw it, I thought. I'm done with politics.

So I didn't exactly take my first political loss well. Remember how horrified I felt when Celso asked Jennifer out for me and she laughed at the prospect? How is it possible to feel that every campaign sign, every glance, every distant laugh, is directed at you?

Of course, that's not the case, but I sure felt like it was. Yet I wouldn't trade in that sense of failure if I had the chance. It taught me how to recover and sharpened my ability to learn from a setback by understanding my weaknesses as well as my strengths. But more important, it impressed on me a very deep, almost spiritual lesson in being open to what the future offers when it doesn't align with expectations. Losing that race hurt, but it helped me run a better, successful campaign for mayor in 2009, which put me on President Obama's radar, eventually leading to my service in his administration. The experience also helped dampen the fear of failure, and the prospect of new, unforeseen opportunities helped offset the pain of defeat.

Before that most public failure of my life, however, I had had to try and fail repeatedly as I learned to build the life I wanted for myself. In 2001 I had won the seat on the San Antonio City Council and become the youngest person elected to that office in San Antonio history at the time. I was indeed young and woefully inexperienced on how to balance my political responsibilities with my professional and personal life.

There is tremendous value in public service, but nobody at that level was doing it for the wages, at least not in San Antonio at that time. San Antonio City Council paid twenty dollars per meeting by city charter, not to exceed $1,040 per year. That America's ninth largest city would pay its elected representatives so little was an anachronism, a measure put into place in the early 1950s as part of the municipal reform movement. Even as San Antonio boomed and the demands on its city council members grew considerably, the salary remained locked.

This was not some benign budgetary matter: it was designed as one method to limit who could reasonably pursue public office. One had to be independently wealthy, supported by a spouse, retired, or, like me, a young professional without kids who was able to juggle both career and public service demands.

I spent mornings at the law firm and afternoons and evenings at my city council office or at neighborhood meetings in my district. I stayed up deep into the wee hours working out plans for the next meeting and trying to reconcile constituents' expectations, my personal experiences as a resident, budgetary considerations, and other council members' proposals.

I had already realized that a full-time job at a law firm and city council duties were too much. But even my three-quarter deal at work wasn't a lasting solution. I lacked experience on how to measure out time, emotions, and energy to avoid burnout, and I tended to get amped up about a policy and put far too much of my time into it. But before I could resolve that situation, my commitment not only to politics but to my entire ethical value system was put to the test.

My employer, Akin Gump, represented Lumbermen's Investment Corporation, an Austin-based developer seeking to develop a 2,861-acre golf complex in San Antonio in partnership with the Professional Golf Association of America. The project, known as the PGA Village, would sit atop some of the last remaining open acreage in the recharge zone of the Edwards Aquifer, which supplied the majority of San Antonio's drinking water. Battles over the aquifer preceded my time in office, and it remained a hot issue. Developers had already used 80 percent of the land over the aquifer, and the need for water had grown so rapidly that the city had to ration it over the summer. The fight against the golf course banded together environmental, anti-tax, and good government activists.

I wasn't inclined to vote for the development as it was proposed, but I couldn't vote on it either way because of my job at Akin Gump. My constituents were solidly opposed to it, but the golf complex had city council support, even though almost all the hydrologists interviewed by the *San Antonio Express-News* foresaw that fertilizers and recycled wastewater could leach into the aquifer below.

Mayor Ed Garza, who had previously represented the district I had won, had close ties with the business community that supported the project. The press pointed out that one of his top contributors owned land close to the complex and could potentially gain from the project, and a member of Garza's campaign team was handling local public relations for Lumbermen's, the developer. Garza was in a tough spot. He traveled to the PGA's headquarters in Florida to see if officials there would find another location to develop, but Lumbermen's threatened to exercise its right to develop nine thousand housing units on that property if the PGA Village wasn't approved. Those units could potentially pollute the aquifer even more, proponents of the project argued.

Lumbermen's wasn't backing down. Similar projects had cost about $150 million; the potential value of this one was $1 billion. As a way of addressing the environmental issues, Lumbermen's offered to donate up to 1,200 acres to the city's aquifer protection program, but that agreement would also allow the creation of a special tax district, and the money collected by that entity would stay within the complex, essentially benefiting the project. Then in the fall of 2001, two more issues arose that I could not vote on because of my employment at the firm.

Clients deserve lawyers dedicated solely to working in their best interests. The public also deserves elected officials whose judgment is not impaired by divided loyalties. I had not thought this through, and now I had to choose between the job that paid $75,000 a year and wasn't fulfilling or the public service job that was rewarding but paid $80 a month.

At the law firm, when I explained that I felt an obligation to resign, one of the attorneys just shook his head.

"Wow, first your brother and now you," he said. Six months earlier, my brother had come to him with a similar dilemma. Joaquin was preparing to run for state representative, and he had learned from me that it was impossible to campaign while holding a full-time job.

The partners at the firm understood where my passion was, and they were gracious when I handed in my resignation letter on January 9, 2002. I sent out a news release announcing my resignation from the firm and my intention to vote on the PGA Village proposal. At the news conference in my cramped city hall office, a reporter asked about my plans to make a living.

"Maybe you'll wait tables on the River Walk?" he suggested jokingly. It was a humorous thing to say, but Mom, who was watching the news with me as the segment aired, had her typical hell-raiser reaction: "You should have told them, 'I'd rather serve tables and serve the people than serve the special interests!'"

Instead of waiting tables, Joaquin and I started our own law firm with a high-school classmate, Andrew Borrego. We rented a modest office in the Deco District and hoped that the ability to manage our own caseload would allow for a better balance between professional and civil work. By the fall of 2002, we were taking on small cases.

My resignation from Akin Gump may have been a pivotal moment for me, but it didn't shift the balance of power on the city council. There were still not enough votes to stop the development, so opponents launched the Smart Growth Coalition, which had an impressive list of allies: the League of Women Voters, Sierra Club, two North Side neighborhood associations, and even the Catholic Church. They argued that the PGA Village would simply create low-wage jobs for some while polluting everybody's water supply.

I thought I'd simply quit Akin Gump and cast my vote, but as I opened the mail in my kitchen one night, I was about to learn the back-alley nature of political engagement. A letter from Lumbermen's lawyer stated that the professional conduct rules for lawyers in Texas protected not just current clients but *former* ones as well, and as a former client, Lumbermen's was rejecting the waiver that would have allowed me to vote. Quitting a high-paying job was informed by my sense of ethics, but this development exposed my lack of real-world political experience. Lumbermen's knew where my vote would fall, so they took it off the table.

The PGA Village quickly became one of the most controversial developments in San Antonio history. A lot of people understandably assume that city council work is boring and unimportant, but fights like this show how vital it is.

Lynnell Burkett, the editorial page editor for the *San*

Antonio Express-News, wrote: "Many think this squabble is about whether a PGA Village would be good for San Antonio. I think the debate is, in fact, over the soul of the city in the new century. I think it is a defining moment for how—not whether—the city will grow and whether it will squander what makes it unique."

A poll by KSAT-TV showed that 61 percent of likely voters opposed the PGA Village. A public forum on the issue went on for two hours, as opponents battered the developer, the city, the water authority, and a local geology professor who was examining the proposal. Not a single person at the forum supported the proposal. These were the people I felt compelled to represent.

I stated that I was going to ask the professional ethics committee of the state supreme court for an official opinion on my ability to vote. Lumbermen's initially stood its ground, but after several weeks of bad press, they relented. I was going to be able to vote.

Then the city's attorney rendered an opinion that if the city council approved a development agreement allowing the resort to be built, that decision could be challenged. If 68,023 registered San Antonio voters signed a petition opposing the decision, the proposal would have to go before all the voters for final action. The people had found a way to be heard and effect change.

Two days after I was cleared to vote, two of the leading opponents of the plan—Communities Organized for Public Service and Metro Alliance—held a Sunday meeting at Sacred Heart Church and invited all eleven members of the city council to attend. Almost a thousand people showed up, but I was the only member of the city council there. It was such a hot-button issue that many members voting for the development essentially hid, but I had quit a lucrative job and fought for the chance to vote on the matter. I wasn't going to stay quiet now.

"I'm voting no," I said simply, becoming the first member of the city council to publicly announce opposition to the PGA Village. "Corporate subsidy...corporate welfare...I don't know if those are reasons enough for giving away sixty million dollars in taxes even if they establish superior safety."

I wanted to be clear on why this was a bad deal for the city. I had been peppered by doubts with my life choices as of late, but my passion ignited that night. Deep down I had felt the pull, but I never consciously understood why I was so drawn to politics. Was it just a result of my upbringing? Ego? A power grab? I'd witnessed all of those things in politicians, but that night I understood why so many others dedicate themselves to this work. As I saw it, I was standing up for what was best for the people I represented. I also felt that I'd passed an important test in politics by leaving my job. I'd chosen integrity over convenience. I was headed in the right direction.

"This PGA Village would really be like another city," I said. "Golfopolis, if you will. That kind of creation I can't support." By then, I had heard from thousands of constituents, and about 75 percent were solidly against it.

The crowd cheered. I had listened and articulated what the majority of my constituents believed about the project.

The city council took up the PGA Village on April 4, 2002, and the chambers were frenetic. Hundreds of people spilled out of the room, waving signs and hollering their position. Outside, a Native American dance troupe performed a traditional number to a pounding drum.

That night I spoke like a lawyer sticking to facts rather than from emotion, but I felt like an activist. I grilled Lumbermen's representatives on their nonsensical position that building homes on the land would be worse than building a massive tourist resort, as if we were being forced to choose the lesser evil. I played audiotapes of a recent state senate committee meeting detailing the abuses of special tax districts.

People began chanting, "Julián! Julián!"

Finally, after hearing from more than two hundred residents over the course of six hours, the council began deliberations, finally taking a vote at nearly three in the morning. I was one of the two members to vote no.

I had lost, which felt like *we* had lost. But we had gone down fighting. If there was one thing I learned from Mom, it was how to take a policy beating and get back up again.

For the first time in politics, I felt I had done my job excellently. I stood up and made sure the people of District 7 were counted, and they were. There was no way this golf complex was going to go up the way it had been envisioned by the developer, without regard to the community's objections or the impact on the environment. There would have to be concessions. Big ones.

Polls showed 56 percent of San Antonio residents disagreed with the council's decision, and the opposition collected 107,000 signatures to overturn the council's vote. The city council had a choice: allow the public to vote or scrap the plan. The council scrapped the plan, and then, totally disregarding the will of the voters, proposed a different deal to finance the special tax district.

That the city council would openly skirt the public's will shocked me. I was so naive that I assumed that politicians put in a good fight but in the end respected the democratic process. Especially in such a public battle. Could elected officials ever truly represent ordinary citizens, given the outsize influence of special interests? The council members who supported the proposal had their reasons, some of them compelling. But despite the public's strong disapproval of the proposal, nearly all the council members had voted for it.

The people were never able to kill the PGA Village, but other factors eventually did. An economic downturn hindered Lumbermen's financing, and in early 2004, a different partnership came to the city with a plan. The new developer had considered many of the public's previous issues with aquifer protection and taxes. They would build two golf courses and a resort and host professional tournaments on the site with stronger environmental protections and without a special taxing district. That was a compromise that worked for both sides, and I voted yes.

The PGA Golf Village had been my longest and most draining campaign. It really taught me how to gather information, listen carefully to all sides, and state clear reasons for voting the way I did. But the most poignant moment for me happened after the first defeat, with the chambers full of political energy. The council had voted at three in the morning and I had walked out at almost four, dead tired.

As I left the building, I saw a poster with my name drawn on it in red marker, folded and lying next to the overflowing trash cans. I had been so focused on dealing with questions about the issue at hand that I never noticed the signs people were waving.

INTEGRITY, CHARACTER, PROMISE. JULIÁN CASTRO FOR MAYOR.

It wasn't Mom's writing—and I checked because, as almost all of us with a mom know, this would be a mom move.

I had no idea who made the sign, but took note of the sentiment. Although we hadn't won, the experience had opened a door in a way that an easy success wouldn't have. They say you can learn a lot about a person by how he loses. People knew I'd fight for them and that I was, at this point in time, doing it to the detriment of my personal life.

The people ended up reelecting me to city council in 2003, and I started my second and final term. I had won considerable political favor with my handling of the PGA Village, but trying to balance my council service with a new law practice, while paying down a substantial student loan and a mortgage, was tough. If I'd stayed with Akin Gump, both payments would have been covered easily, with money left over. And if I hadn't bought a house right out of law school, I would have been able to maneuver financially a lot more freely. But I never regretted making the decision to resign from the firm, and I remain proud that I made that judgment call when I was so young. I had ample political cachet—and almost zero in my bank account.

Joaquin, meanwhile, had moved back in with Mom to save money and live in the right district as he prepared to run for state representative. My brother had not paid me much rent, but every contribution counted. The reporter who had asked me about waiting tables was older and probably understood financial burdens better than I did at the time. I thought he was just being a smartass, but on reflection I think his question was a somewhat honest one.

The answer to that question was a law firm that barely made money. Joaquin and I had survived for a while on small civil litigation cases, but ultimately closed the practice a little over a year after we started. A lot of the blame was mine. My pursuit of public service occupied most of my time and creative energy, leaving less focus on developing business for the firm. Joaquin's focus was also elsewhere, as he dedicated more and more time to his campaign for the Texas House of Representatives, which he won in 2002. Like some virus sweeping though the Castro household, we were all getting the political bug, except Joaquin was smarter and went for the job that paid six hundred dollars a month instead of eighty.

Some people are drawn to public office in part because they believe it will help their job prospects. In many states, Texas in particular, part-time legislators have stayed on the payroll of companies that saw them as useful development assets. They didn't have to do much real work; their contribution was to be door openers. I saw these types of arrangements as having the serious potential to compromise one's integrity, even cause one to hold back instead of take on powerful monied interests. The upside for me was that I kept my independence from such influence. The downside was that I would continue for the next few years to perform a harder and harder balancing act.

In the decade since Joaquin and I left for college, San Antonio had grown to just over one million people. Like the country in general, it was also diverse. Annexation had expanded it to more than four hundred square miles, large enough to encompass the city of Chicago or Dallas.

In years past, San Antonio had relied on tourism as its primary economic driver, with the Alamo and the River Walk being two of Texas's most popular sites. But now health care was the largest economic engine. Although the city had changed since Joaquin and I left, I was convinced that San Antonio had not kept pace with other progressive cities, which were laser-focused on enhancing their local economy by improving educational achievement.

After I left Akin Gump, financial reality set in. Stupidly, I ignored the increasing number of overdue mortgage bills, leaving them unopened and stacked in a drawer out of sight as I struggled to clear enough at our little firm to keep my head above water. After not receiving my mortgage payment for too many months, however, the bank started foreclosure proceedings. I was lucky in that I could get a good-paying job more easily than most, but if I wanted to keep my house and what was left of my credit rating, then I had changes to make. I was hired by the law firm of Gonzales, Hoblit & Ferguson and was right back where I had started, working at a law firm part time so that I could serve the people full time. But now, there were no conflicts of interest in the type of businesses the firm represented.

Having achieved some stability, I decided to run for mayor. The job paid only four thousand dollars a year, but I had found a balance with work and public service. Joaquin, fresh from his victory, was my first campaign adviser, and my circle grew to include a wide range of community and political leaders.

My advisers identified a few weaknesses. A major one was a lack of support from the business community. Even though my primary focus was on economic development and creating jobs, I had a reputation for opposing development. Another issue was my age. I was thirty but I looked even younger, and that youthfulness would be used against me.

My two main opponents posed a stark contrast with me. Carroll Schubert was a Republican who had also been on the city council. Middle-aged with a heavy Texas accent, he and I had polar-opposite voting records on the council. I believed in using government as a tool to improve people's lives, and he believed in small government. Phil Hardberger, a former appellate court judge, was a longtime Democrat.

Hardberger began his attack indirectly by saying that San Antonio needed "adult leadership" at city hall. It was an especially good play because it tied me to the current mayor, who was thirty-six and not terribly popular.

Then there was Twingate, which made the national news and the Associated Press before fizzling out.

The controversy started at the River Parade, a massive event held every April on the San Antonio River. The parade is televised, and almost a quarter-million people gather along the banks to watch it. It's the family-friendly Texas version of Mardi Gras. Political candidates usually attend events like this with their family, and since I wasn't married yet, I often brought my brother. The city council had its own float, and I was scheduled to be on it with other council members, waving to the crowd. At the last minute, I realized that I had a scheduling conflict, but Joaquin wanted to go on the float still, and we thought nothing of it. He notified my council, but nobody corrected the list of float participants for the parade announcer, and he identified Joaquin as me.

Joaquin heard himself announced as me, but he couldn't yell that he wasn't me to two hundred thousand people, so he just kept waving. We still didn't think anything of it, but an honest mistake and confusion makes for a catchy conspiracy story, and the national news outlets picked it up. We hadn't planned it, there was no diabolical scheme to capitalize on our likeness, and there wasn't much political gain to be gotten out of the confusion. Joaquin and I were interviewed on programs like *The Early Show* on CBS, and the story's initial spark fizzled out as soon as we simply explained what had happened.

But Hardberger had jumped on it, hinting at some sort of deception that Joaquin and I had planned. "If you're eighteen years old and having a date, it might be a youthful prank when you swap out your brother," he said. "But when you're running for mayor of a city with 1.3 million people and sending in your brother as an impersonator, I do see a problem with it."

In the May general election, I came in first place with 42 percent of the vote, followed by Hardberger at 30 percent and Schubert at 26. That set up a June runoff election between Hardberger and me. As the runoff election neared, the polls had me down by three points, but I'd never lost in politics, and I had confidence I could win what was clearly a very close contest.

When the early polls closed on June 7, 2005, I had 41.5 percent of the vote. Like a balloon my confidence suddenly popped. I tried to hide it from Erica, but she is a hard one to BS. My veneer of confidence was peeling right in front of her as we drove into the parking lot outside the building where I would await the results.

The press was there already, and a microphone had been set up onstage for an announcer to declare the results. My team had already assembled for the evening. Mom, Joaquin, and Erica were there, along with a few of my Harvard pals who had been with me through two council elections. A lot of people in the crowd were wearing Castro for Mayor T-shirts. Some held signs with red, white, and blue letters that read One City, One Destiny.

My campaign manager came in and showed me some new data.

"Look," he said, pointing to the numbers rising sharply from the earlier 41 percent. "We're closing in." He saw the spark in my eyes from the adrenaline. It wasn't over.

He squeezed my shoulder. "It's going to be a long night."

The clock struck twelve, and five minutes later, the mayoral seat that I could almost feel myself sitting in transformed into something else altogether.

Hardberger, 51.5 percent. Castro, 48.5 percent.

That's when the reporter came over and began asking questions about the campaign and my plans, and I mumbled, "I think I'm done with politics."

*   *   *

After my defeat, I turned my attention to building my new law practice and getting married. Well, as most people who get married know, there is usually not that much for the groom to do except nod and be told where to stand. Perfect for me, since I was more than happy to hand off to Erica the organization for this pageantry.

And sometimes, life finds ways to balance things out. Joaquin was a visiting professor at St. Mary's University, working multiple jobs to supplement his small political income. We had spoken about my new firm, and he saw how my approach this time was making a difference. It took a while, since our previous effort had flamed out, but as his visiting professorship ended, we both knew what was going to happen. Over burgers, I finally said it.

"Just come over. Let's stop messing around."

"Do we call it Castro and Castro?" he asked. "Castro Squared?"

"That's horrible. You're fired."

The mayoral loss was hard to accept, but it made me appreciate what I did have. I was going to marry an amazing woman (who continues to keep me in check), and I did well enough with the civil cases I'd taken on that I could pay off my student loan debt and stay current on my mortgage.

Erica and I were married on June 30, 2007, at the Little Flower Basilica, the church where Mamo had worshipped with the García family when she was a girl. In the weeks before our wedding ceremony, I kept getting the same question over and over again.

"Are you nervous?" I must've been asked a hundred times. I wasn't at first, but by the time our wedding day arrived I'd been asked the question so many times that I actually became nervous. As I waited with Joaquin in an antechamber of the church before the ceremony, I had visions of passing out, like one of the grooms I'd seen hit the deck in a grainy home video from *America's Funniest Home Videos*. I snapped out of it later, though, when I saw that Erica was having trouble staying cool as we knelt at the altar in front of Father Eddie Bernal. She kept trying to fan herself and began fidgeting with her veil. It was almost ninety degrees outside and the church had no air conditioning. She was about to pass out! I motioned to Father Eddie Bernal, who was performing the service, and he had two chairs brought over for us to sit on. Thankfully, Erica felt better after five minutes, and the rest of the ceremony went beautifully.

"Thank you for that, honey," I teased Erica afterward. "You saved me from passing out first!"

Erica moved in with me after we got back from our honeymoon in Los Cabos.

Now it was time to start fixing the fixer-upper I had bought seven years earlier. I needed no encouragement to rip out the stained and worn carpet that had been in the house when I bought it. Erica and I briefly debated the faux wood paneling that lined the walls—perhaps it would come back in style in another fifteen years?

Erica is not one for flashy shows of wealth, but she did have limits. She shook her head at the paneling, then pointed to the popcorn ceilings that were probably sprayed with asbestos. "Those are getting scrapped," she declared.

Stability in my life allowed me to consider getting back into politics. In 2009, two years into our marriage, I reflected back on our first date. I had told Erica about my plans to be mayor, and I still connected with that nervous young guy digging into his nachos. The sting of the loss had faded, and very valuable lessons had been learned from it. I could see that I had made mistakes that cost me the election, but I also was convinced I could win if I ran again.

That year was one of major life changes. Erica's water broke three months after I declared my intention to run again, and on March 14, 2009, our daughter, Carina, was born. The feeling was something I had never experienced. From the moment I held her for the first time, I loved my baby girl more than anything else in the world. Erica and I were excited to be new parents and although learning how to be good parents was more than a little stressful, I think it also brought the two of us closer together. By this time, I was also a little bit frantic, since Election Day was only two months away.

Two years earlier, I had become friends with Mike Beldon, a local businessman who'd served as Hardberger's campaign treasurer, as well as with others who'd previously supported my opponent. I think they were surprised when I began talking to them about why they thought I had lost instead of showing hostility. It never occurred to me to be angry — I accepted all the blame for my campaign loss and was curious as to their experienced, outside view of things I did wrong. They were sometimes brutally honest but also very helpful.

Ultimately, their input and a broad-based coalition of supporters helped me win my second mayoral campaign in 2009.

On my first day as mayor, I sat at my desk and wrote a letter to two-month-old Carina on my new letterhead:

Dear Carina,

Today is my very first day as mayor of San Antonio. I wanted you to be the first constituent to receive a letter from me, since you are my favorite.

One day when you are older, you will understand how happy I feel today. A dream that I have had for many years has come true. And I am going to make sure I do exactly what your grandmother Rosie taught me I should—help people.

I don't know what your dreams are. You're young and they're far off still. But I do know that your mom and I will do everything we can to make your dreams come true. Your happiness is our happiness. I love you. And as happy as I am to be called mayor, I'm more thrilled thinking of the day you'll call me Daddy.

Love always,

Daddy

I was exactly where I'd wanted to be, with a beautiful family and in a position to make a real difference in my hometown. I couldn't imagine changing anything—until a certain president came calling.

Chapter Eleven

I'm at a stoplight when my cell phone rings.

Private number.

That's almost always a reason to send a call straight to voicemail, but somebody who had a blocked number had said to expect a call. Still, it was almost nine at night, pretty late for that kind of business call.

I paused, holding a rice bowl in my hand from the Panda Express that I'd just left. I'd just carefully opened the bag so as not to spill any of the sauce before pulling out of the parking lot.

"Mr. Mayor, how are you?"

There is no mistaking President Barack Obama's voice.

"Mr. President!"

There's something regal and at the same time humorous about how elected officials address other elected officials. It's obviously a sign of respect for the office, similar to the military, but also carries a hint of theatrics that I haven't found elsewhere in adult life.

It was 2014. President Obama was five years into his historic presidency, and I was serving my third term as mayor of San Antonio. I had learned so much from my time as a city council member that my tenure as mayor seemed quite productive. As the youngest mayor of a top fifty city who had won reelection with nearly 82 percent of the vote, and as a young Latino, I emerged on the president's radar and was often invited to White House events and various other functions. I'd managed my nerves well enough not to throw up before delivering the keynote address at the 2012 Democratic National Convention. But it wasn't as if we were chatting on any regular basis.

However, just a few days earlier we'd been at the Lyndon Baines Johnson Library and Museum at the University of Texas, Austin, to celebrate the fiftieth anniversary of Johnson's signing of the Civil Rights Act. The significance of having the nation's first African American president commemorate such an iconic piece of legislation was not lost on either of us.

We spoke backstage briefly before he gave his speech. It was mostly casual talk, but as I turned to walk away, he said, "I'm going to call you about something."

President Obama's speech that day resonates now as much as it did in 2014. As he spoke, I knew full well that neither he nor I would have reached the places we had in public service without the passage of the Civil Rights Act.

"To all the members of Congress, the warriors for justice, the elected officials, and community leaders who are here today—I want to thank you," the president began. "Today, as we commemorate the fiftieth anniversary of the Civil Rights

Act, we honor the men and women who made it possible. Some of them are here today. We celebrate giants like John Lewis and Andrew Young and Julian Bond. We recall the countless unheralded Americans, black and white, students and scholars, preachers and housekeepers—whose names are etched not on monuments, but in the hearts of their loved ones, and in the fabric of the country they helped to change."

At one point he tied together the struggle from the start of our country to today, showing how we still need to fight for progress. "LBJ was nothing if not a realist. He was well aware that the law alone isn't enough to change hearts and minds. A full century after Lincoln's time, he said, 'Until justice is blind to color, until education is unaware of race, until opportunity is unconcerned with the color of men's skins, emancipation will be a proclamation but not a fact.' "

He departed quickly after his speech, and as I walked back to my car, I started wondering what the president wanted to talk to me about. Was I in trouble?

I had criticized the administration two days earlier at the same forum. During a panel discussion about the prospects for progress on immigration reform, a moderator had asked me how I felt about the Obama administration's approach on immigration.

"I don't agree with it," I said, and went on to explain how I disagreed with the number of deportations and believed the administration could do more to protect law-abiding established immigrant families who had been here for many years. I was the mayor of a city, not a member of Congress with direct influence on immigration policy, so in theory my thoughts didn't really count for much.

But President Obama's selection of me as the 2012 convention's keynote speaker gave my comments on immigration a substantive and symbolic weight. After all, the nucleus of the speech was how my grandmother immigrated here and pursued the American dream. I didn't regret my answer at the forum, but I now wondered if I was going to hear about it from Obama.

"How are you?" I said on speakerphone.

"I'm fine," he answered. "How are you? Probably doing a little better than me when you check the sports page. The Spurs look like they're going to make another run."

The San Antonio Spurs were looking strong again this year, and the president's passion for basketball was common knowledge.

"It's not a bad time to be a Texan," I agreed.

"How are things in San Antonio?"

"Great. We're competing to get Tesla's battery factory built here. We think San Antonio has a decent shot."

"I had Elon Musk over the other day—that's a sharp guy. Good luck with that," the president said. "But what I'm calling about is an upcoming opening at the Department of Housing and Urban Development. As much as we'd both like to see you as governor of your state, it's probably not ready yet."

I concurred. The state was still heavily Republican and had been for two decades.

"It hasn't been announced yet," he continued, "but Shaun Donovan is leaving HUD and going to move over to OMB [Office of Management and Budget], and I'm calling to see if you're interested in taking his old role on."

President Obama had been very complimentary to me over the years, but I had been expecting a very different call, so I was slightly disoriented. This was a lot to process on an empty stomach.

"That sounds like something I'd be inclined to do," I said.

"Glad to hear that."

I looked at the remainder of my Panda Express. My appetite was now overwhelmed by excitement.

"Can I get back to you by the end of the week? It would be a big change, and there are some folks I'd have to talk to, namely my wife, Erica."

"Absolutely," President Obama said. "I know exactly how that goes. We'll talk again soon."

"Take care," I said.

"You too."

He hung up.

I pulled into the driveway, scooped my Panda Express back into the bag, and walked inside the house. My daughter, Carina, was already asleep, and I bent down to kiss my wife. Erica is the most supportive person in my life. We still live in that small fixer-upper I bought after graduating from law school. The same house she saw me nearly lose in foreclosure. I've done a lot better in the years since, but Erica has been as content during the times when I had only a little as when I had a lot.

We have a fantastic life together, but politics occupies this in-between zone for her. She doesn't love it and she doesn't hate it, but she engages in it because she knows it matters and because it makes me happy.

"President Obama just called and offered me a spot in his cabinet. I'd be running HUD."

Erica put her fork down and thought for a moment. Once again, it was a lot to process. I was a sitting mayor and we had settled into a life with a daughter and a home and school and steady jobs.

"Really?" she said. "It didn't matter that you turned him down a year ago?"

No *specific* position had been offered, but in January 2013 the president had called when I was also driving, and we had a very brief conversation about a position opening in his administration that had something to do with transportation.

"Julián, I know you're happy where you're at, but if you ever want to join my administration, let me know," the president had said.

I was deeply honored, but I immediately declined the offer. In San Antonio we'd just passed Pre-K 4 SA, a sales tax initiative that expanded high-quality, full-day prekindergarten in the city. I was riding high as mayor and wanted to stick around to see the program get implemented successfully in the fall of 2013.

Of course, I excitedly told Erica about the conversation with the president. When I explained that I had turned down his apparent offer to join his administration because I wanted to make sure Pre-K 4 SA was firmly anchored into the community, she agreed that I'd made the right decision. In a way, it was the same type of reasoning that led me to resign from Akin Gump back in my city council days, except that this time I had a partner in my decision. Erica holds a master's in educational leadership, and she was a major source of inspiration in the Pre-K 4 SA program.

Then I began to second-guess my flat-out rejection of the president's offer, especially without probing further. Had I come off as disrespectful? I wanted to let the president know that I sincerely appreciated his overture and that, if an opportunity arose to work with him in the future, I hoped he'd keep me in mind. I contacted the White House for a meeting with the president. It was a few days before the inauguration, which I had been invited to attend, so I knew we'd be in the same area at least around that time.

We met in the Oval Office the day after his inauguration. I had seen a lot in politics, but I have no problem admitting that I felt like a wide-eyed kid as I was escorted into the room for the first time.

That said, the Oval Office is kind of small.

Old photos and video footage had made it seem much more expansive. But the room in front of me was smaller than the corner offices in Manhattan law firms. The earthy tones of the carpet, furniture, and curtains gave the room a calm atmosphere. Did each president get new carpeting? I thought I remembered Ronald Reagan standing on a bold, power-red carpet, and Bill Clinton walking on a royal-blue one. This was much more chill, the wall a shade of light brown, and like nature you felt awed by the surrounding atmosphere. It didn't need to exclaim anything via strategized color combinations — it had confidence in its power. Small was no longer the leading descriptive.

Did I just write a paragraph about carpet? Anyway, I was

pretty impressed. But it was a lesson in how President Obama operates in life. He doesn't put much stock in pageantry and drumming up insignias of power to convey authority. Obama was and remains at ease with himself, and that gave him a solidity that conveyed authority more genuinely and effectively than any of the usual supports politicians use.

"Mr. Mayor!" boomed that unmistakably presidential voice as I walked in. He projected such a sense of powerful warmth that my instinctual inner response was disbelief. *I turned this guy down?* He welcomed me with a hug, and, as a photographer snapped away, we settled into chairs that faced the *Resolute* desk.

I thanked him for his interest in bringing me on board, careful not to call what we had discussed over the phone a specific job offer. Then I explained why I wanted to stay in San Antonio at the moment, describing my Pre-K 4 SA program and how much it meant to me given my family's experiences. I detailed how the voters had approved it in November and how we were about to implement it in the fall. If I left, I feared the disruption would doom it to failure.

"I want every child to get a great start to their education," I said, "and I think this program will help with that." President Obama had not had a gilded childhood. We could relate over a father leaving and the presence of a strong mother and grandmother in our lives. Joaquin and my story was not that far off from the president's.

He nodded. "I understand."

I thanked him again for the responsiveness of his White House team whenever we'd called with a request from San

Antonio, and pledged my support on anything else that I could help with. We spoke for several minutes about the future—his second term, the years ahead for me—and then, as we got ready to wrap up our meeting, I thanked him again for the opportunity to be the keynote speaker at the Democratic National Convention.

"Thanks again for your confidence in me," I said. "I look forward to continuing to work with you as mayor."

Then I left him with a thought. "If, in the future, the Secretary of Education slot opens up, I hope you'll consider me for that role."

Obama grinned. "I'll keep that in mind."

Another message was delivered in a much subtler manner later that year. In a meeting with members of the Congressional Hispanic Caucus that Joaquin attended, the president was pressed as to why there weren't more Latinos in high-ranking positions.

He looked at the group and pushed back. "We all know a certain mayor who could've written his own ticket," he said, "but he thinks he's going to be governor of Texas."

And now, roughly a year later, he had reached out to me with another seat in his administration, one that he knew I also felt passionate about, considering my family's history. And, just for good measure, he had given a realistic forecast of the political winds surrounding the Texas governorship in 2014. I'm not sure if he remembered that Pre-K 4 SA had been successfully implemented by this time, but he did seem to be suggesting that now could be the time for a step up to the next level.

"Maybe he respected *why* you turned down the first position he offered?" Erica said. I looked at Erica, considering the connection she'd made to my previous rebuff.

"Well, it wasn't explicitly offered," I replied, and Erica smiled.

"Maybe you are right," I said. "I actually think that my meeting after turning down the job made more of an impression." I sat down with her at the table and we reflected on my first meeting at the Oval Office. "I had already given the keynote speech, so I knew he had confidence in me, but our conversation allowed us to delve into why I'm in public service and what I'd like to accomplish for people through it."

Erica pushed the chair away and hugged me.

"We'd have to move to DC," I said to my wife, whose hands were already full with her teaching job and with three-year-old Carina running around.

Erica looked at me. It's a good feeling when your spouse is happy and proud. Then I watched as she mentally sorted out living sixteen hundred miles away from family and friends — Erica had never lived outside of San Antonio.

My nomination as HUD secretary was announced in late May 2014 at the White House, and when I returned to San Antonio, I spoke with my mayoral staff. I'd known most of them for many years, and I owed them a great deal for their support and for helping realize Pre-K 4 SA, one of my proudest achievements in my years of public service. I felt better about leaving my post as mayor because there was concrete evidence that I had done my job well. San Antonio was doing better than peer cities economically, and voters had just given me a huge vote of confidence at the ballot box. Together we had found ways to address big, inveterate challenges and begin solving them. I can honestly say that if my career in public service had ended then, I would have been satisfied, since making San Antonio better was why I'd gone into politics in the first place.

The path that leads to education, which directly leads to opportunity, can be vastly different from one person to the next. Mamo, for instance, had no path at all, while some of my classmates at Stanford and Harvard traveled an established route. As I spoke to parents and students as mayor, I began formulating a plan that would cut more of a well-worn path for *everybody* to follow, regardless of what neighborhood one came from.

Tending that path would not be cheap—Pre-K 4 SA would could cost tens of millions of dollars annually. The prospect of raising taxes is hardly ever popular, but it's often easier to seek a tax hike for stadiums, roads, or an airport than to ask for one that invests in people directly.

My job was to explain why Pre-K 4 SA was a good investment for everybody. I tried to demonstrate that the entire city of San Antonio would benefit, regardless of whose kids attended the program. If we raised taxes by one-eighth of a cent, at an estimated cost of eight dollars per year for each family right now, that investment would pay off many times over in the future with the better job opportunities that come to a well-educated workforce.

Irrespective of party lines, many businesspeople in San Antonio helped me develop and campaign for Pre-K 4 SA, including Charles Butt, the owner and CEO of H-E-B, and General Joe Robles, CEO of San Antonio–based insurance giant USAA, both of whom co-chaired the task force that recommended pursuing Pre-K 4 SA at the ballot box. Their support was crucial to winning over support from moderates and conservatives.

In November 2012, 54 percent of San Antonio voters approved funding for Pre-K 4 SA.

On election night, I felt as though I were honoring Mamo. The program didn't have her name on it, but for me the motivation started with her when she shared her struggles and life with me. She never got over how limited her life had been because she'd never finished school. Still, Mamo had become one of my greatest teachers, and as a result she helped influence an entire generation of children in the city she grew up in.

There were other accomplishments I felt proud of as well. We'd launched Café College, a one-stop center in downtown San Antonio that offered free admissions and financial-aid advice, because we'd discovered that the student-to-counselor ratio in our local public high schools was 420 to 1. We'd steered the local municipal utility to embrace renewable energy, including a deal for 400 megawatts of solar power and a $50 million investment in the University of Texas at San Antonio for renewable energy research. We'd focused tremendous time and attention working to improve long-neglected neighborhoods in the city's urban core, winning several federal grants to lift up San Antonio's underserved East Side. And, to provide a long-term vision for the city's prosperity, we'd started SA2020, a community-based effort that brought thousands of San Antonians together to set specific goals for the city to achieve by Friday, September 25, 2020, ten years after its launch.

I'd chosen public service because I wanted to see others in

my hometown get the kind of opportunities that come with a good education, and now, with Pre-K 4 SA operating and funded through at least 2020 and Café College in place to fill an important gap, I felt as though I'd put the city on a better track. I was ready for a new challenge.

A few days after the Panda Express presidential call, I dialed the White House and passed along a message to the president.

He called back later that day.

"Mr. Mayor!"

"Mr. President. I'd be interested in taking on the HUD role."

"Glad to hear that, and I'll get the ball rolling on this end."

Within a week, FBI investigators began an exhaustive background check that lasted almost a month. My entire personal, financial, and political history was scrutinized, and many of my friends and colleagues going back to high school were interviewed.

About a month after President Obama asked me to join the administration, Erica and I received even more exciting news. She was pregnant with our second child. When we found out we were going to have a boy, I was ecstatic. "Now we'll have the complete set—a girl and a boy," I joked with Erica. She was already five months pregnant when we moved into the Woodley Park neighborhood, just a fifteen-minute drive from the HUD offices. In December, Erica would give birth to Cristián, a beautiful baby boy who would bring more joy and chaos to our daily lives in the way only a newborn can. I was back again in Washington, but this time with a real job and a place of my own. The shift from city council to mayor felt like walking up some steep stairs to another floor, but leveling up from mayor to the president's administration sometimes felt like stepping into a space shuttle that took off before I'd buckled in.

Having the president and vice president introduce you in front of a line of cameras and reporters at the White House is a few steps beyond surreal. There's a part of me that remains a kid from the West Side of San Antonio and looks at all this in awe. And I never want to lose that sense of wonder and joy, because it helps balance the more difficult aspects of the job.

The president opened by talking about how hard the housing crises had hit America and what HUD had done in the past five years to improve the situation. "Now, here's the problem: When you're good at your job, people always want you to do even more," President Obama said. "That's why I'm nominating Shaun to be the next director of the Office of Management and Budget, and to take his place at HUD, I am nominating another all-star who has done a fantastic job in San Antonio over the past five years, Mayor Julián Castro."

He went on to describe Shaun and me as "proven leaders" and "proven managers." "They are going to be effective, and most importantly, they've got huge heart," he said. "They're involved in public service for the right reasons." Then he spoke about Mamo. That didn't sink in until much later, but it was amazing to realize that the president of the United States had stood behind a podium and told the world about her life: "Julián's grandmother came to this country from Mexico. She worked as a maid, worked as a cook, worked as a babysitter—whatever she had to do to keep a roof over her family's head. And that's because for her, and generations of Americans like her, a home is more than just a house. Home is a source of pride and security and a place to raise a family and put down roots...and maybe one day the kid grows up in that home and is able to go on to get a great education and become the mayor of San Antonio and become a member of the president's cabinet."

Then he said, in Spanish that was pretty damn good, *"Julián ha vivido el Sueño Americano."*

Julián has lived the American dream.

Some kids stand in front of the bathroom mirror and sing into a comb, imagining themselves performing onstage. Others hold a shampoo bottle and recite Oscar acceptance speeches. Now, Mamo and I were part of a speech that neither one of us would ever have dreamed of.

After Shaun spoke, I walked up to the podium, thanked the people of San Antonio, the president and vice president, and my family. "My brother, Joaquin, and I grew up on the West Side of San Antonio," I said, "taking public transportation and living in rental homes as we grew up. And it was there that both of us got a sense of what is possible in America, and an understanding that just because you were of modest means does not mean that your aspirations or your opportunity ought to be limited. And it certainly means that you can have the talent to succeed and achieve the American dream."

The printed program delved into my family history and included a comment about Joaquin and me that always struck me as funny. (Joaquin was a member of Congress and already living in DC.) "Together they make the most high-ranking identical twins ever to serve in government."

At the nomination press conference, President Obama had

said, "I hope that the Senate confirms them both without games and without delay." The Senate confirmed me on July 9, 2014, by a vote of 71 to 26.

That summer, Erica, Carina, and I settled into our new home. While it's hot and humid at that time, the capital is vibrant and designed in a very walkable manner, so Erica would start the day with long walks with Carina and end up at the zoo or one of the many world-class museums. Carina also began attending the Oyster Bilingual School, which was right next door.

HUD's mission is to expand housing opportunities for Americans of modest means and help revitalize communities across the United States. It also focuses on urban development by giving grants to help develop infrastructure and stimulate local job growth. Finally, the department also works to ensure the housing market is free from discrimination.

The HUD building, located about two miles from the White House, looked like something that needed assistance from the department it housed. Ten stories tall, it was built in the stark brutalist style of architecture that was popular in the 1960s, when the building was constructed. It reminded me of images I'd seen on TV of old Soviet government buildings, stultifyingly drab. Its proximity to a highway had coated the flat gray concrete with soot, like tartar on teeth. Worse still, some of its windows were boarded up, awaiting replacement.

Jack Kemp, the ninth HUD secretary, is said to have described his office building as "ten floors of basement."

The broken-down vibe continued inside. Elevators would often stall, and at least once a week we'd hear about somebody getting stuck inside. The lift shuddered and jerked every trip I made up to my tenth-floor office. When I walked into my barren office for the first time, I was greeted by what may have been the ugliest wood paneling in Washington. I don't why, but I cannot escape wood paneling—my fixer-upper house had it, my mayor's office had it, and now my HUD office had it. I could have requested a renovation and stripped the wood paneling, but at this point it seemed to be a lucky charm in my life, so I left it.

Months later, I received a bid to acid wash the outside of the building, and when it came in at $650,000, I laughed out loud. That money could obviously do a lot more good elsewhere. Within reason, what HUD's offices looked like mattered little to the people HUD was trying to help.

Running a department that helps people struggling with poverty and homelessness is a critical responsibility of our government, and perceived frivolous spending casts doubt on that mission. When I traveled to nearly one hundred cities during my time at HUD, I flew coach on more than ninety-five of those flights, even when offered an automatic upgrade into first class. Public servants need to be aware of how optics can instantly change a person's perception of the government's role in their lives. I was always keenly aware of whose money I was spending.

The soot stayed put, and so did the wood paneling. We had far bigger, more pressing matters to deal with.

When I became HUD secretary, the country, and the world, was still recovering from the financial crises triggered by the bursting of the housing bubble. HUD had served as a critical source of assistance for millions of Americans. The loss of homeownership, the resulting deterioration of neighborhoods from the foreclosure crisis, and the lack of new housing supply led the country into a rental affordability crisis, and the inadequate support from Congress to meet demand put tremendous stress on the HUD bureaucracy. Back in 1981, HUD had more than sixteen thousand employees; by 2014, with demand for its services having increased dramatically in the previous three decades, the department was half that size. Still, I knew there was a lot of potential to increase opportunity for tens of millions of people HUD directly interacted with. With a budget of more than forty-six billion dollars and fifty-four field offices around the country, I wanted to start helping as many people as possible.

If you look at my efforts on city council, as mayor, and as head of HUD, you'll find all have one major thrust: the expansion of opportunity. I had learned as a mayor that strong leadership is the most important ingredient in trying to solve tricky and complex problems. I had brought some trusted advisers over from San Antonio, including Frances Gonzalez, who had been my boss when I'd interned in the Office of Special Projects; Robbie Greenblum, who had served as my chief of staff; Jaime Castillo, who had run communications for the office; and Lani Esparza and Stacie Weber, who had worked on scheduling. I had a chief of staff, deputy chief of staff, and about twenty-five core people on my executive team. I had to pick three or four things to focus on while my staff kept me updated on matters within their scope of authority. Over the next two and a half years, we focused not only on distributing grants but also on generating real-world solutions to provide more opportunities to disadvantaged Americans.

Times had changed since Joaquin and I had flipped over a Macintosh mouse to try and solve it like some Rubik's Cube. By 2014, access to the internet was a dividing line, a digital set of railroad tracks separating the haves from the have-nots.

Access to the internet is such a necessary part of life today that many Americans would be shocked to discover how many citizens still don't have it. In fact, the vast majority of public-housing residents had no access to broadband at home. My team and I identified that as a gap that needed to be closed as quickly as possible. Lack of internet at home affected how kids could do their homework, how they could apply to college, and how their parents could look for and respond to job opportunities.

In the modern world, how do you look for jobs when you can't regularly search job sites or post your résumé on LinkedIn? How do you access breaking news? How do you specifically pursue an interest, watch videos, and read articles that broaden and inspire? People get frustrated at a coffee shop that doesn't offer free Wi-Fi—imagine that 24/7.

In order to close this gap we created ConnectHome. We partnered with internet service providers, housing authorities, and nonprofits to offer free or heavily discounted internet access to people in public housing. In July 2015, the president traveled to the Choctaw Nation in Durant, Oklahoma, to launch the ConnectHome pilot program in twenty-seven cities and one tribal nation. Over at HUD, I spoke with the press, and my team posted videos on the White House website and You-Tube channel to show people how to sign up for the program. In the months after its launch, ConnectHome had connected thousands of families to the internet, a measurable, concrete victory for them and for HUD.

I also came to realize how integral mayors were to the success of so many of HUD's programs, particularly the Mayors Challenge to End Veteran Homelessness, a special priority for the president and First Lady. We worked with mayors and the Veterans Administration to locate and identify veterans in need. HUD vouchers were made available through the VA's case management system in conjunction with housing authorities across the community. Homeless veterans were entitled to a voucher that provided assistance for three years so long as they contributed 30 percent of their income to rent. Thirty-six communities eventually reached "functional zero" in veteran homelessness, which means that there was a system in place that had identified and offered vouchers to every veteran in need. That didn't mean that there were no homeless veterans in these communities—a person could become newly homeless on a given day, and some individuals did not want to participate in the program—but all the ones that did want help received it. Overall, veteran homelessness had dropped 47 percent by the end of Obama's second term.

As we worked to end homelessness, I was constantly learning about the lives of the people HUD helped. I met James, a man in his fifties who had lived on and off the streets for more than a decade. He was adjusting to life in his new Philadelphia apartment and was doing well. He explained how the stability was allowing him to build a more structured and secure life. He was looking for a job, eating regularly, finding a network of friends and support groups—and struggling with some unexpected issues.

"I keep forgetting my key!" he said.

I didn't understand.

"I haven't had to keep track of a house key in so long that I've forgotten it over five times already when I leave my apartment."

There was one major initiative I worked on that was long overdue. In 1968, Congress passed the Fair Housing Act to prohibit discrimination in the housing market. Under the act, the secretary of HUD had an obligation to "affirmatively further fair housing." The problem was that, almost fifty years later, HUD had never defined what that meant or how it would go about "affirmatively furthering fair housing." We changed that in the summer of 2015, when we released the Affirmatively Furthering Fair Housing Rule. Its aim was to hold cities, counties, housing authorities, and others that received taxpayer funding through HUD accountable for ensuring that their policies and investments promoted equal housing opportunity. We aimed to end the "other side of the tracks" dynamic that took hold in post-WWII urban communities in which racial minorities were packed into the "bad" areas of town and thereby deprived of access to good jobs, good schools, and good amenities. HUD developed mapping tools for communities, and governmental entities receiving HUD assistance had to submit plans every five years and explain how they were using the funds.

I traveled to Chicago—the city where Martin Luther King Jr. had led the Chicago Freedom Movement five decades earlier to open up better access to housing opportunity—to announce the initiative. Paraphrasing President Obama, I said that people's zip codes should never prevent them from reaching their aspirations. *The Nation* published a piece on HUD's new rules, and it included a personal story as well as some alarming data on how location affects not only opportunity but all aspects of life.

Speaking about her hometown, writer Angela Glover Blackwell wrote:

> For instance, in zip code 63106, a distressed neighborhood in northern St. Louis, 96 percent of residents are Black and 52.5 percent of families live in poverty— more than three times the national poverty rate. A child born and raised here is expected to live only 69 years— 10 years below the national average—and attend schools deemed so substandard that the state was forced to take them over in 2007. Drive 20 minutes southwest and you reach Clayton (zip code 63105), an affluent and predominately white suburb of St. Louis, where residents live on average 16 years longer, and their children attend schools in one of the best districts in Missouri.
>
> This is what modern-day segregation looks like.

Angela started her article by saying how she had grown up in circumstances similar to mine, except in St. Louis rather than San Antonio, but she pointed out something shocking that HUD works hard to fix: how different zip codes highlight a frightening difference in life expectancy, one that rivals the gap between first- and third-world countries. In light of that disparity, HUD's impact can be much greater than just finding people housing, distributing vouchers, and fighting homelessness. When HUD succeeds, it can make a difference in quality and quantity of life.

As the first AFFH plans came rolling into HUD from cities across the country, I felt pride in knowing that because of our efforts, many lower-income families, including many families of color, would be able to live in neighborhoods with better job and educational opportunities. By requiring local communities to get serious about addressing unequal opportunity, we could ensure broader and more inclusive prosperity. This was something worth fighting for.

Shortly after I took office, the Senate switched over to a Republican majority, giving Republicans full control of Congress, and the climate for executive agencies worsened. Unfortunately, testifying in front of a committee had degenerated. What used to be a platform to increase understanding and public accountability was now often an arena in which to score political points in a broadcast setting. The fact that people's lives were sometimes considered fodder for some sort of theater was off-putting but not altogether surprising. Unfortunately, that's the direction too much of our nation's politics have gone in — less substance and more shouting.

Washington hadn't always been this way. Many of HUD's successes, from the Community Development Block Grant program to the Federal Housing Administration, enjoyed bipartisan support and were developed with insight, creativity, and empathy. I appreciated the instances when members from the other side of the aisle supported HUD's work, crossing partisan lines. Mario Diaz-Balart and Susan Collins were two Republicans who helped maximize HUD's impact on people in need.

Regardless of party, it is important to avoid the temptation of reflexively blaming people living in poverty for being poor and therefore unworthy of society's help. Are there abuses in the system? Of course, but that seems to be a product of the human condition that transcends income levels. The benefits I saw people experience when their lives improved with HUD assistance *vastly* outweighed any abuses I saw while at HUD, and those abuses had infinitely less impact than the abuses the financial industry had levied on our economy.

President Obama had clearly succeeded in increasing opportunity for all Americans, bringing the economy back from the Great Recession and expanding health care to millions more Americans. But the summer of 2016, wistfulness descended on the administration with the realization that a historic president would soon complete his final term in the office. The game of musical chairs in Washington, meanwhile, had begun. Who would become the next president? What would the new cabinet look like?

As my tenure at HUD wound down, much of my time was spent cementing policies in place and preparing for the next appointee. I felt happy about the opportunities we'd helped make possible for Americans who didn't have much to begin with, and I was optimistic that it would continue. Many of the people I'd met along the way during my tenure at HUD had made me hopeful but also keenly aware that we still had a lot of work to do as a nation. In San Diego I'd visited the site of an apartment building that was being renovated to house homeless veterans. The developer of the project introduced himself as a veteran. He said that, like the people his housing would serve, he had been homeless once too, and this project was his way of ensuring that others had the same opportunity for a second chance in life that he'd gotten. On the Pine Ridge Indian Reservation, I'd seen some of the most extreme poverty I'd ever witnessed. At one house, I met a family that lived among seventeen people in a dilapidated, one-story home in which two families shared a dirt-floor basement, their privacy maintained by clotheslined bedsheets. Their stories also put my own into perspective. I realized that, as much as opportunity had made a difference in my life, I'd been fortunate to get it, because meaningful opportunity seemed to be in shorter and shorter supply. I used to think that if everyone worked hard things would work out okay for them. But that wasn't true anymore. We needed to restore the formula of rewarding hard work with meaningful opportunity that had been at the core of the American dream that Mamo and so many others had pursued.

Which direction we'd go in as a nation would soon be determined by the presidential election in November 2016. With Hillary Clinton taking on Donald Trump, I felt good about our chances to make history and then make progress.

Epilogue

On November 9, 2016, millions of unsinkable expectations sank. There are tragedies that are more devastating, of course, but the sight of thousands of people crying or staring straight ahead, dazed, in a New York City arena scrambles one's sense of normalcy.

The evening before, I was at the Jacob Javits Convention Center for Hillary Clinton's election night watch party. I had front-row seats to the electoral disaster in more ways than one. Hillary Clinton had been expected to win the presidency, and although no official list was ever released, I'd learned in the summer that I was one of ten potential running mates the Clinton campaign was vetting.

The vice-presidential selection process is one of the weirdest parts of American politics. It's not like school PE class, where you line up out in the open and see who gets picked first. Everything about it is done in a hush-hush, wink-wink manner. It happens almost entirely behind closed doors, and there's a tradition—sometimes it felt like an obligation—of active prospects denying they're being vetted or even that they're interested in being vetted. The selection itself is made as undemocratically as possible, by the nominee alone. Still, the mechanics of the process provide clues as to what the candidate's team is thinking. The vetting lasts only for about a month, but it is intense. Clinton campaign chairman John Podesta had called me in the middle of June. I picked up the phone, and he got right to the point. "Julián, would you like to be a part of the vetting process?"

John is a seasoned pro, and he did what he could to downplay expectations. There were a number of candidates being vetted, he said, and Hillary would make a decision based on who she believed could best help her govern effectively. It was a call I had expected. The media had begun speculating on possible running mates years before the campaign even began, raising the possibility of a Clinton-Castro ticket two days after my keynote address at the 2012 Democratic National Convention. After my appointment to HUD, the buzz only increased, as pundits wondered if President Obama was giving me the Washington experience I'd need to fill the running-mate role come election time. Then it reached a fever pitch when the *Washington Post* reported in the fall of 2014, shortly after my arrival in Washington, that I'd had dinner with Bill Clinton at the Clintons' Washington home.

A Clinton-Castro ticket had a certain political logic to it. Presidential campaigns often "balance" their ticket along demographic, geographic, and ideological lines. The 1960 Democratic ticket of John Kennedy and Lyndon Johnson was a classic case—a young man and an experienced one, a New Englander and a Texan, a progressive and a moderate. To some extent, Hillary and I fit this pattern. She had experience and I was a fresh face, she hailed from New York and I came from Texas, and we shared progressive values. Adding fuel to the fire was the conventional wisdom that Democratic presidential victories would be assured for many years to come if Latinos could be mobilized.

President Obama's ability to garner more than 70 percent of the Latino vote had been crucial to his reelection victory over Mitt Romney in swing states like Colorado, Florida, Nevada, and Virginia. Romney's loss marked the fourth time in five presidential cycles that the Republican candidate had lost the popular vote. Soon after, the Republican National Committee commissioned an analysis, dubbed an "autopsy," to assess what had gone wrong in 2012 and to make recommendations on how Republicans could become more competitive in the years ahead. It urged the Republican Party to improve its relationship with Latinos. With this in mind, more than a dozen Senate Republicans had joined with Democrats to pass comprehensive immigration reform legislation in the spring of 2013. The legislation, which passed with sixty-eight votes, eventually failed to become law when the Speaker of the House, John Boehner, refused to allow it to be taken up for a vote on the House floor. Still, the conventional wisdom for 2016 was set: Latinos now had the ability to change the political tide pulling the next president.

But Trump hit the established world of American politics like a rogue wave, obliterating almost all political precedent.

He'd begun his campaign by suggesting that most undocumented Mexican immigrants were rapists and murderers, then later accused an American-born federal judge who was presiding over fraud claims against Trump University of being unable to do his job because of his Mexican heritage. The Clinton campaign, like most political observers, assumed that Trump's words would spark a backlash in the Latino community and push them into Hillary's camp at an unprecedented rate, obviating the need to appeal to them directly. Clinton-Castro didn't make quite as much sense then.

Still, I was confident I had a lot to contribute to the ticket besides my heritage.

"Sure. I'm interested," I told John.

Within seventy-two hours, I was being vetted, swept into the wide-ranging political interrogation that all potential VPs go through. All ten candidates were assigned two lawyers and a team of investigators to start digging. Veteran Washington attorney Jim Hamilton oversaw the process. The investigators reviewed all my speeches and media appearances and had me complete a form with 129 questions. Then I sat through a four-hour interview and a two-hour follow-up interview at a Washington law office. Within three weeks the vetting team had produced two full binders detailing my political and personal history, including information about my personal finances and my family members. I even had a physical to prove that I was in good health.

Throughout the process, I was unsure how I ranked among the other potential candidates. The only way I knew that I was still in the running was when someone from the team would contact me with additional questions. Then, in mid-July, I met privately with Hillary at her home in Washington. The meeting lasted about an hour, and although it was pleasant, I had a good sense well before I walked in that I wasn't the pick.

I'd been stumping for Hillary in a handful of swing states during the primary and had introduced her at a couple of events, but our relationship was still very much in the development stage during the vast majority of her campaign. We spoke briefly—nothing too long or involved—whenever we saw each other at one of these campaign events. Even so, I could tell that she was well prepared to serve as president. I'd never met anyone with deeper knowledge about policy than Hillary, and she seemed unflappable and genuinely interested in using the power of the office to benefit the lives of those who don't often have a strong voice in our democracy.

She also had a reputation for being politically cautious.

Would Clinton take a chance on a young running mate, especially with the way things turned out for Sarah Palin, John Edwards, and Dan Quayle? She probably figured that since she was way ahead, there was no point in taking a risk when she didn't have to.

Near the end of July, it was announced that she had picked Tim Kaine. He was a great choice, a passionate advocate for better opportunity for all Americans, who had experience as both a governor and a senator.

Dan Balz, the longtime *Washington Post* political columnist, called me when the news leaked, wanting to get my thoughts on Kaine's selection and to ask about my future. I told him that Kaine was a strong choice and noted how well organized and thorough the selection process had been. I was disappointed but remained optimistic about my own future. "I can see that in life, the road turns," I reflected, "and you don't know how things are going to work out, and that oftentimes things can work out for the better." Indeed, I had already learned that unanswered prayers could lead to better things in the long run. Losing the mayor's race in 2005 had worked out for the better, since my election in 2009 held the prospect of serving more than four years as mayor and doing so with Barack Obama in the White House instead of George W. Bush, which led to public service beyond San Antonio.

After the VP selection, I met John at his home in Washington to discuss other roles I might play in a Clinton administration. I couldn't be sure exactly what the years ahead would hold, but I felt confident that they would include more public service. As the election drew closer, I continued campaigning for Hillary, visiting Iowa, Colorado, and Ohio, as well as Austin, Houston, and Dallas.

In late October, I received an invitation to attend the election night festivities. I arrived in New York on Election Day and went to my hotel a mile from the venue. The city was buzzing even more than usual, and there was a crackle of energy in the air. Although both candidates hailed from the state, in New York City people were overwhelmingly pro-Hillary, and from Brooklyn to midtown to the Bronx, everybody seemed poised for a major celebration.

I met friends for dinner around eight o'clock. The restaurant was full of Hillary supporters, and the anticipation felt more like New Year's Eve than the night of an election. When the early results started coming in, my phone pinged me and I took a quick glance. Although only a smattering of minor precincts were reporting at that time, I was surprised at how they tilted in Trump's favor.

But it was still early, and like most of the country, I simply assumed that there was no way a person who had conducted himself as terribly as Trump had would have a real chance of winning.

After we finished dinner, I decided to go back to the hotel before heading over to the Clinton campaign celebration. I flopped down on the bed and turned on the TV to watch more results come in. I figured I'd walk over to the center in an hour to celebrate.

But as votes were tabulated from Florida, Pennsylvania, Ohio, and other swing states, my nerves began to fray. Most were too close to call at first, but then Trump began winning states he was expected to lose. By around ten that night, it was obvious that he had a real chance of winning the election.

My phone rang, and, seeing Joaquin's name, I answered.

"What is going on?" he blurted out. I could tell by his voice that he was as dumbfounded as I was.

"Who the hell knows," I shot back, "but at least it's not over yet. She's still got a chance."

As the night wore on and the unbelievable became believable, I couldn't pull myself away from the phone or TV. I waited at the hotel, hoping for things to turn around before heading over to the convention center.

By ten thirty, although it still wasn't clear who was going to win the election, Trump had taken the lead in the electoral college. I put on my shoes and jacket and got into the car.

It was a quick drive over to the Javits Center, where I showed security my pass and made my way to one of the two large VIP rooms. Mounted on one wall was a massive screen showing MSNBC's coverage of election returns. Some of the most famous celebrities in the world huddled in a small group and stared at the screen, reluctant to believe the unbelievable. The murmuring rose as Hillary's supporters tried to make sense of what was unfolding in front of them.

After twenty minutes, I walked out onto the main floor and waded into a pool of thousands of Democrats whose hope was being drained out of them by the thought of what a Trump presidency would really mean for the country and the world. When a journalist asked for my thoughts on the prospect of a Trump administration, I told him I hoped that he would govern differently from how he had campaigned, that the awesome responsibility of the nation's highest office would sober him up, and that he would work on behalf of all Americans.

At a little after one in the morning on November 9, I headed back to my hotel. Once there, I lay down and turned on the TV again. I saw John Podesta addressing the Javits Center crowd, saying Hillary wasn't done and that we should all go home and let the votes be counted. In other words, Hillary wasn't conceding yet, but we all knew that moment was on the horizon and approaching quickly.

I fell asleep with the TV still on.

Three hours later I woke up, still dazed from the night before. I looked at the TV to see if something miraculous had happened since I had last checked, but what I encountered made me feel like I was back in a dream state: Donald Trump was president of the United States of America.

What had just happened?

I got ready to leave New York and return to Washington, knowing things would change drastically for the country, likely in a bad way, especially for the most vulnerable Americans. My family and I would be fine, but things would change quite a bit for us as well.

I called Erica, eager to hear her voice and talk about what the future would look like for us. We had made loose plans to stay in Washington for the next few years. She had gone back home to San Antonio with the kids in late June, and I had moved into a studio in the same Woodley Park apartment building. We had decided to start looking for a more permanent base in the capital over the next few months, when job prospects solidified.

Now everything was different.

"Change of plans, huh?" I told Erica. "Looks like we're going to be in Texas."

"I can't believe what happened last night," she said. "But being in San Antonio sounds nice," she added, happy to stay close to home.

On January 19, the day before Trump's inauguration, I flew back to San Antonio to begin post-Washington life with my family. Erica had resumed her work in public education, returning to the school district she'd graduated from two decades earlier. I took a role as a visiting fellow lecturing at the Lyndon B. Johnson School of Public Affairs at the University of Texas at Austin. Both of us are enjoying more quiet time with Carina and Cristián.

Since the election, I've been incredibly proud of how people have shown resistance to the new administration, whether it be to the travel ban targeting Muslims, the corruption defining this administration, or the tax cuts benefiting the rich at the expense of everyone else. Many Americans have told me how, the morning after the election, they made a vow to start participating in politics more regularly, to show consideration for others, to simply represent in their everyday lives the ideals that America was built on. This resolve would be put to the test when the cruelty of Trump's policy separating migrant families at the border came into full view.

The morning after the demonstration at the Ursula processing and detention center, I sat in a federal courthouse in Brownsville, Texas, about sixty miles away, as undocumented immigrants apprehended at the border made their first appearance before a judge. Forty-eight individuals, men and women from Mexico and Central America, stood near the front of the courtroom with headsets, listening to a translation of the proceedings. The judge called out their names one by one and asked them a series of questions about their background. They all looked spent, resignation and anxiety etched on their faces. Some of them had been separated from their children. A short, middle-aged woman with dark-brown skin and black hair made the sign of the cross, as if to steel herself against what was to come.

I remembered the way Mamo would bless Joaquin and me as we left the house every morning for school. *"Que Dios los bendiga,"* Mamo would call out, making the sign of the cross with her hand toward us.

I felt sad for the souls in front of me in that courtroom. They had journeyed a long way from home in search of safety and a better life in America, all to no avail. But at the same time, I was grateful for how my own family's journey had turned out.

In September 2015, Pope Francis visited the White House. As Joaquin and I sat in the audience, I could imagine Mamo sitting there with us, quiet and respectful with her black veil on, the way she liked to be in church. I thought about how proud she would be that her grandsons, one a member of the president's cabinet and the other a member of Congress, were here in this moment. After he finished his remarks, the pope joined President Obama and First Lady Michelle Obama in a small reception room nearby. Members of the cabinet were invited to greet the pope. As I approached the pope in the receiving line, the president, standing next to him, introduced me.

"This is the secretary of Housing and Urban Development," he told the pope.

"Julián Castro, *secretario de Vivienda,*" I introduced myself in Spanish, and we exchanged a few more words briefly, long enough for me to express my gratitude for his visit. After a photographer memorialized the moment, I moved on to shake hands with the First Lady.

"Thank you so much for having us here and for the opportunity you've given me," I told her.

"Oh, thank *you,*" she said, smiling warmly. She leaned in. "You've come a long way, haven't you?" And then, before I could say anything, she added, "We've all come a long way."

Embrace your own unlikely journey.

About the Author

Julián Castro served as the sixteenth secretary of Housing and Urban Development under President Barack Obama from 2014 to 2017. He was the mayor of San Antonio, Texas, from 2009 to 2014 and delivered the keynote address at the 2012 Democratic National Convention.